SIXTH EDITION

MICROSOFT® VISUAL BASIC® PROGRAMS TO ACCOMPANY *PROGRAMMING LOGIC AND DESIGN*

BY JO ANN SMITH

COURSE TECHNOLOGY
CENGAGE Learning™

Australia • Brazil • Japan • Korea • Mexico • Singapore • Spain • United Kingdom • United States

COURSE TECHNOLOGY
CENGAGE Learning™

Microsoft® Visual Basic® Programs to Accompany *Programming Logic and Design*, Sixth Edition
Jo Ann Smith

Executive Editor: Marie Lee

Acquisitions Editor: Amy Jollymore

Senior Product Manager: Alyssa Pratt

Development Editor: Mary Pat Shaffer

Content Project Manager: Jennifer Feltri

Art Director: Marissa Falco

Proofreader: Suzanne Ciccone

Indexer: Sharon Hilgenberg

Compositor: Integra

For product information and technology assistance, contact us at
Cengage Learning Customer & Sales Support, 1-800-354-9706

For permission to use material from this text or product, submit all requests online at **www.cengage.com/permissions**
Further permissions questions can be e-mailed to
permissionrequest@cengage.com

Library of Congress Control Number: 2010928662

ISBN-13: 978-0-538-74625-0
ISBN-10: 0-538-74625-4

Course Technology
20 Channel Center Street
Boston, MA 02210
USA

Cengage Learning is a leading provider of customized learning solutions with office locations around the globe, including Singapore, the United Kingdom, Australia, Mexico, Brazil, and Japan. Locate your local office at: **international.cengage.com/region**

Cengage Learning products are represented in Canada by Nelson Education, Ltd.

For your lifelong learning solutions, visit **course.cengage.com**
Visit our corporate Web site at **cengage.com**.

Some of the product names and company names used in this book have been used for identification purposes only and may be trademarks or registered trademarks of their respective manufacturers and sellers.

Any fictional data related to persons or companies or URLs used throughout this book is intended for instructional purposes only. At the time this book was printed, any such data was fictional and not belonging to any real persons or companies.

Course Technology, a part of Cengage Learning, reserves the right to revise this publication and make changes from time to time in its content without notice.

The programs in this book are for instructional purposes only.
They have been tested with care, but are not guaranteed for any particular intent beyond educational purposes. The author and the publisher do not offer any warranties or representations, nor do they accept any liabilities with respect to the programs.

Printed in the United States of America
1 2 3 4 5 6 7 14 13 12 11 10

Brief Contents

Contents

iv

vi

CHAPTER 5   Writing Programs Using Loops **74**

CHAPTER 6   Using Arrays in Visual Basic Programs **96**

ix

Preface

Microsoft® Visual Basic® Programs to Accompany Programming Logic and Design, Sixth Edition (also known as, *VB PAL*) is designed to provide students with an opportunity to write Visual Basic programs as part of an Introductory Programming Logic course. It is written to be a companion text to the student's primary text, *Programming Logic and Design, Sixth Edition*, by Joyce Farrell. This textbook assumes no programming language experience and provides the beginning programmer with a guide to writing structured programs and simple object-oriented programs using introductory elements of the popular Visual Basic programming language. It is not intended to be a text-book for a course in Visual Basic programming. The writing is non-technical and emphasizes good programming practices. The examples do not assume mathematical background beyond high school math. Additionally, the examples illustrate one or two major points; they do not contain so many features that students become lost following irrelevant and extraneous details.

The examples in *VB PAL, Sixth Edition* are often examples presented in the primary textbook, *Programming Logic and Design, Sixth Edition*. The following table shows the correlation between topics in the two books.

VB PAL, Sixth Edition	Programming Logic and Design, Sixth Edition
Chapter 1: An Introduction to Visual Basic and the Visual Basic Programming Environment	Chapter 1: An Overview of Computers and Logic
Chapter 2: Variables, Constants, Operators, and Writing Programs Using Sequential Statements	Chapter 2: Working with Data, Creating Modules, and Designing High-Quality Programs Chapter 3: Understanding Structure
Chapter 3: Writing Structured Visual Basic Programs	Chapter 2: Working with Data, Creating Modules, and Designing High-Quality Programs Chapter 3: Understanding Structure

(continues)

(continued)

VB PAL, Sixth Edition	Programming Logic and Design, Sixth Edition
Chapter 4: Writing Programs that Make Decisions	Chapter 4: Making Decisions
Chapter 5: Writing Programs Using Loops	Chapter 5: Looping
Chapter 6: Using Arrays in Visual Basic Programs	Chapter 6: Arrays
Chapter 7: File Handling and Applications	Chapter 7: File Handling and Applications
Chapter 8: Advanced Array Techniques	Chapter 8: Advanced Array Concepts, Indexed Files, and Linked Lists
Chapter 9: Advanced Modularization Techniques	Chapter 9: Advanced Modularization Techniques
Chapter 10: Creating a Graphical User Interface (GUI) Using the Visual Studio Integrated Development Environment (IDE)	Chapter 10: Object-Oriented Programming Chapter 11: More Object-Oriented Programming Concepts Chapter 12: Event Driven GUI Programming, Multithreading, and Animation

Organization and Coverage

Microsoft® Visual Basic® Programs to Accompany Programming Logic and Design, Sixth Edition provides students with a review of the programming concepts they are introduced to in their primary textbook. It also shows them how to use Visual Basic to transform their program logic and design into working programs. The structure of a Visual Basic program, how to compile and run a Visual Basic console program, and introductory object-oriented concepts are introduced in Chapter 1. Chapter 2 discusses Visual Basic's data types, variables, constants, arithmetic and assignment operators, and using sequential statements to write a complete Visual Basic program. In Chapter 3, students learn how to transform pseudocode and flowcharts into Visual Basic programs. Chapters 4 and 5 introduce students to writing Visual Basic programs that make decisions and programs that use looping constructs. Students learn to use Visual Basic to develop more sophisticated programs that include using arrays, control breaks, and file input and output in Chapters 6 and 7. In Chapter 8, students learn about sorting data items in an array and using multidimensional arrays. Passing parameters to procedures is introduced in Chapter 9. Lastly, in Chapter 10, students learn about the Visual Studio Integrated Development Environment (IDE), and gain some experience in creating a Graphical User Interface (GUI) and writing event-driven programs. Students also learn to write programs that include programmer-defined classes.

This book combines text explanation of concepts and syntax along with pseudocode and actual Visual Basic code examples to provide students with the knowledge they need to implement their logic and program designs using the Visual Basic programming language. This book is written in a modular format and provides paper-and-pencil exercises as well as lab exercises after each major topic is introduced. The exercises provide students with experience in reading and writing Visual Basic code as well as modifying and debugging existing code. In the labs, students are asked to complete partially pre-written Visual Basic programs. Using partially pre-written programs allows students to focus on individual concepts rather than an entire program. The labs also allow students to see their programs execute.

VB PAL, Sixth Edition is unique because:

- It is written and designed to correspond to the topics in the primary textbook, *Programming Language and Design, Sixth Edition*.

- The examples are everyday examples; no special knowledge of mathematics, accounting, or other disciplines is assumed.

- It introduces students to introductory elements of the Visual Basic programming language rather than overwhelming beginning programmers with more detail than they are prepared to use or understand.

- Text explanations are interspersed with pseudocode from the primary book, thus reinforcing the importance of programming logic.

- Complex programs are built through the use of complete examples. Students see how an application is built from start to finish instead of studying only segments of programs.

Features of the Text

Every chapter in this book includes the following features. These features are both conducive to learning in the classroom and enable students to learn the material at their own pace.

- Objectives: Each chapter begins with a list of objectives so the student knows the topics that will be presented in the chapter. In addition to providing a quick reference to topics covered, this feature provides a useful study aid.

- Figures and illustrations: This book has plenty of visuals, which provide the reader with a more complete learning experience, rather than one that involves simply studying text.

- Notes: These notes provide additional information—for example, a common error to watch out for.

- Exercises: Each section of each chapter includes meaningful paper-and-pencil exercises that allow students to practice the skills and concepts they are learning in the section.

- Labs: Each section of each chapter includes meaningful lab work that allows students to write and execute programs that implement their logic and program design.

Acknowledgments

I would like to thank all of the people who helped to make this book possible, especially Mary Pat Shaffer, Developmental Editor, whose expertise and attention to detail have made this a better textbook. She also provided encouragement, patience, humor, and flexibility when I needed it. Thanks also to Alyssa Pratt, Senior Product Manager, and Amy Jollymore, Acquisitions Editor, for their help and encouragement. I am grateful to Jennifer Feltri, Content Project Manager, and Vidya Muralidharan, of Integra Software Services, for overseeing the production of the printed book. It is a pleasure to work with so many fine people who are dedicated to producing quality instructional materials.

I am dedicating this book to my son, Tim and his son, my grandson, William. Both add great dimension and joy to my life.

Jo Ann Smith

Read This Before You Begin

To the User

Data Files

To complete most of the lab exercises, you will need data files that have been created for this book. Your instructor will provide the data files. You also can obtain the files electronically from the Course Technology Web site by connecting to *www.course.com*, and then searching for this book title.

You can use a computer in your school lab or your own computer to complete the lab exercises in this book.

Solutions

Solutions to the Exercises and Labs are provided to instructors on the Course Technology Web site at *www.course.com*. The solutions are password protected.

Using Your Own Computer

To use your own computer to complete the material in this textbook, you will need the following:

- Computer with a 1.6 GHz or faster processor
- Operating system:
  - Windows XP (x86) with Service Pack 3 - all editions except Starter Edition
  - Windows Vista (x86 & x64) with Service Pack 2 - all editions except Starter Edition
  - Windows 7 (x86 and x64)

- Windows Server 2003 (x86 & x64) with Service Pack 2 - Users will need to install MSXML6 if not already present

- Windows Server 2003 R2 (x86 and x64)

- Windows Server 2008 (x86 and x64) with Service Pack 2

- Windows Server 2008 R2 (x64)

- Architectures: 32-Bit (x86) and 64-Bit (x64) (WOW)

- RAM:

  - 1024 MB

  - 1.5 GB if running in a Virtual Machine

- 3 GB of available hard-disk space

- 5400 RPM hard drive

- DirectX 9-capable video card that runs at 1024 x 768 or higher display resolution

- DVD-ROM Drive

This book was written using Microsoft Windows Vista and Quality Assurance tested using Microsoft Windows Vista and Windows 7.

Updating Your PATH Environment Variable

Setting the PATH environment variable allows you to use the Visual Basic compiler (vbc) and execute your programs without having to specify the full path for the command.

To set the PATH permanently in Windows 7:

1. Click the **Start** button in the lower left corner of your Desktop.

2. Select **Control Panel**, click **System and Security**, and then click **System**.

3. Select the **Advanced system settings** link. Click **Yes**, if necessary.

4. In the System Properties dialog box, select the **Advanced** tab, if necessary, and then click the **Environment Variables** button.

5. Select **PATH** or **Path** in the User variables or System variables section, click **Edit**, and then edit the PATH variable by adding the following to the end of the current PATH:

    ;C:\Windows\Microsoft.NET\Framework\v4.0.30128

Note that it is important to include the semicolon (;) at the beginning of the path, preceding C:\. You may have to replace the "v4.0.30128" with the version number you have installed. You also may have to substitute the drive letter of the partition you are working on if it is not *C:*. A typical PATH might look like this:

C:\Windows;C:\Windows\System32;
C:\Windows\Microsoft.NET\Framework\v4.0.30128

6. When you are finished editing the PATH variable, click **OK**.

7. Click **OK** on the Environment Variables dialog box.

8. Click **OK** on the System Properties dialog box.

9. Close the System window.

To set the PATH permanently in Windows Vista:

1. Click the **Start** button in the lower left corner of your Desktop.

2. Select **Control Panel** and then select **Classic View**, if necessary.

3. Double-click **System**.

4. Select the **Advanced system settings** link. Click **Continue**, if necessary.

5. In the System Properties dialog box, select the **Advanced** tab, if necessary, and then click the **Environment Variables** button.

6. Select **PATH** or **Path** in the User variables or System variables section, click **Edit**, and then edit the PATH variable by adding the following to the end of the current PATH:

   ;C:\Windows\Microsoft.NET\Framework\v4.0.30128

   Note that it is important to include the semicolon (;) at the beginning of the path, preceding C:\. You may have to replace the "v4.0.30128" with the version number you have installed. You also may have to substitute the drive letter of the partition you are working on if it is not *C:*. A typical PATH might look like this:

   C:\Windows;\C:Windows\System32;
   C:\Windows\Microsoft.NET\Framework\v4.0.30128

7. When you are finished editing the PATH variable, click **OK**.

8. Click **OK** on the Environment Variables dialog box.

9. Click **OK** on the System Properties dialog box.

10. Close the System window.

To set the PATH permanently in Windows XP:

1. Click the **Start** button in the lower left corner of your Desktop.

2. Select **Control Panel** and then double-click **System**.

3. In the System Properties dialog box, select the **Advanced** tab, and then click the **Environment Variables** button.

4. Select **PATH** or **Path** in the User variables or System variables section, click **Edit**, and then edit the PATH variable by adding the following to the end of the current PATH:

   ;C:\Windows\Microsoft.NET\Framework\v4.0.30128

   Note that it is important to include the semicolon (;) at the beginning of the path, preceding C:\. You may have to replace the "v4.0.30128" with the version number you have installed. You also may have to substitute the drive letter of the partition you are working on if it is not *C:*. A typical PATH might look like this:

   C:\Windows;C:\Windows\System32;
   C:\Windows\Microsoft.NET\Framework\v4.0.30128

5. When you are finished editing the PATH variable, click **OK**.

6. Click **OK** on the Environment Variables dialog box.

7. Click **OK** on the System Properties dialog box.

8. Close the System window.

Capitalization does not matter when you are setting the PATH variable. The PATH is a series of folders separated by semicolons (;). Windows searches for programs in the PATH folders in order, from left to right.

To find out the current value of your PATH, at the prompt in a Command Prompt window, type: **path**.

To the Instructor

To complete some of the Exercises and Labs in this book, your students must use the data files provided with this book. These files are available on the Course Technology Web site at *www.course.com*. Follow the instructions in the Help file to copy the data files to your server or standalone computer. You can view the Help file using a text editor such as WordPad or Notepad. Once the files are copied, you may instruct your students to copy the files to their own computers or workstations.

Course Technology Data Files

You are granted a license to copy the data files to any computer or computer network used by individuals who have purchased this book.

An Introduction to Visual Basic and the Visual Basic Programming Environment

After studying this chapter, you will be able to:

◎ Discuss the Visual Basic programming language and its history

◎ Recognize the three types of Visual Basic programs

◎ Explain introductory concepts and terminology used in object-oriented programming

◎ Recognize the structure of a Visual Basic program

◎ Complete the Visual Basic development cycle, which includes creating a source code file, compiling the source code, and executing a Visual Basic program

2

You should do the exercises and labs in this chapter only after you have finished Chapter 1 of your book, *Programming Logic and Design, Sixth Edition*, by Joyce Farrell. This chapter introduces the Visual Basic (VB) programming language and its history. It explains some introductory object-oriented concepts, and describes the process of compiling and executing a Visual Basic program. You begin writing Visual Basic programs in Chapter 2 of this book.

The Visual Basic Programming Language

Visual Basic is a programming language that you can use to create interactive Web pages and to write Web-based applications that run on Web servers. **Web servers** are the computers that "serve up" content when you request to view Web pages. An online bookstore and an online course registration system are examples of **Web-based applications**. Visual Basic is also used to develop Windows-based **stand-alone enterprise applications** (programs that help manage data and run a business).

What makes Visual Basic especially useful is that it is an object-oriented programming language. The term **object-oriented** encompasses a number of concepts explained later in this chapter and throughout this book. For now, all you need to know is that an object-oriented programming language is modular in nature, allowing the programmer to build a program from reusable parts of programs called classes, objects, and methods.

When Visual Basic was introduced by Microsoft in 1991, it was described as the perfect programming language because it allowed programmers to easily create applications that include a **graphical user interface (GUI)**. A GUI allows users to interact with programs by using a mouse to point, drag, or click.

Three Types of Visual Basic Programs

Visual Basic programs can be written as Web applications, Windows applications, or console applications. A **Web application** is a program that runs on the World Wide Web and is available to end users on any platform (e.g., Windows, Mac, Linux). A **Windows application** is a program, such as Microsoft Word or Excel, that runs on a Windows system. A **console application** is a program, without a GUI, that executes in a console window and produces text-based output. In Chapters 1 through 9 of this book, you write console applications. Visual Basic programmers often use the Microsoft Visual

Studio Integrated Development Environment (IDE) when they write programs. In Chapter 10, you learn to use the IDE to create Visual Basic Windows applications that include a simple GUI.

Writing console applications is a good way to learn a language because when you are working on one, you don't have to be concerned with a GUI. Console applications allow you to focus on the syntax of the language and the language constructs, such as how and when you use selection and looping statements. (You'll learn about selection and looping statements later in this book.)

An Introduction to Object-Oriented Terminology

You must understand a few object-oriented concepts to be successful at reading and working with Visual Basic programs in this book. Note, however, that you will not learn enough to make you a Visual Basic programmer. You will have to take additional Visual Basic courses to become a Visual Basic programmer. This book teaches you only the basics.

To fully understand the term *object-oriented*, you need to know a little about procedural programming. Procedural programming is a style of programming that is older than object-oriented programming. **Procedural programs** consist of statements that the computer runs or **executes**. Many of the statements make calls (a request to run or execute) to groups of other statements that are known as procedures, modules, methods, or functions. These programs are known as "procedural" because they perform a sequence of procedures. Procedural programming focuses on writing code that takes some data (for example, quarterly sales figures), performs a specific task using the data (for example, adding up the sales figures), and then produces output (for example, a sales report). When people who use procedural programs (the users) decide that they want their programs to do something slightly different, a programmer must revise the program code, taking great care not to introduce errors into the logic of the program.

Today, we need computer programs that are flexible and easy to revise. Object-oriented programming languages, including Visual Basic, were introduced to meet this need. In object-oriented programming, the programmer can focus on the data that he or she wants to manipulate, rather than the individual lines of code required to manipulate that data (although those individual lines still must eventually be written). An **object-oriented program** is made up of a collection of interacting objects.

An **object** represents something in the real world, such as a car, an employee, or an item in an inventory. An object includes (or **encapsulates**) both the data related to the object and the tasks you can perform on that data. The term **behavior** is sometimes used to refer to the tasks you can perform on an object's data. For example, the data for an inventory object might include a list of inventory items, the number of each item in stock, the number of days each item has been in stock, and so on. The behaviors of the inventory object might include calculations that add up the total number of items in stock and calculations that determine the average amount of time each item remains in inventory.

In object-oriented programming, the data items within an object are known collectively as the object's **attributes** or **properties**. You can think of an attribute or property as one of the characteristics of an object, such as its shape, its color, or its name. The tasks the object performs on that data are known as the object's **methods**. (You can also think of a method as an object's behavior.) Because methods are built into objects, when you create a Visual Basic program, you don't always have to write multiple lines of code telling the program exactly how to manipulate the object's data. Instead, you can write a shorter line of code, known as a **call**, that passes a message to the method indicating that you need it to do something.

For example, you can display dialog boxes, scroll bars, and buttons for a user of your program to type in or click on simply by sending a message to an existing object. At other times, you will be responsible for creating your own classes and writing the code for the methods that are part of that class. Whether you use existing, prewritten classes or create your own classes, one of your main jobs as a Visual Basic programmer is to communicate with the various objects in a program (and the methods of those objects) by passing messages. Individual objects in a program can also pass messages to other objects.

When Visual Basic programmers begin to write an object-oriented program, they first create a class. A **class** can be thought of as a template or pattern for a group of similar objects. In a class, the programmer specifies the data (attributes/properties) and behaviors (methods) for all objects that belong to that class. An object is sometimes referred to as an **instance** of a class, and the process of creating an object is referred to as **instantiation**.

To understand the terms *class*, *instance*, and *instantiation*, it's helpful to think of them in terms of a real-world example—baking a chocolate cake. The recipe is similar to a class, and an actual cake is an object. If you wanted to, you could create many chocolate cakes that are all based on the same recipe. For example, your mother's birthday cake, your sister's anniversary cake, and the cake for your neighborhood bake sale all might be based on a single recipe that contains the same data (ingredients) and methods (instructions). In object-oriented programming, you can create as many objects as you need in your program from the same class.

The Structure of a Visual Basic Program

When a programmer learns a new programming language, the first program he or she traditionally writes is a Hello World program—a program that displays the message "Hello World" on the screen. Creating this simple program illustrates that the language is capable of instructing the computer to communicate with the outside world. The Visual Basic version of the Hello World program is shown in Figure 1-1.

```
Module HelloWorld
    Sub Main()
        System.Console.WriteLine("Hello World.")
    End Sub
End Module
```

Figure 1-1   Hello World program

At this point, you're not expected to understand all the code in Figure 1-1. Just notice that the code begins with the word Module. Module is a special word, known as a **keyword**, which is reserved by Visual Basic to have a special meaning. A Module is one of the possible packages into which you can place code that you want to compile and execute. The Module keyword tells the Visual Basic compiler that you are beginning the creation of a Module and that what follows is part of that Module. The name of the Module is up to you; however, to make your program easier to maintain and revise later, take care to choose a meaningful name. Because this program is written to display the words "Hello World." on the user's screen, it makes sense to name the Module HelloWorld. The keywords End Module on the last line of Figure 1-1 mark the end of the Module.

On the second line in Figure 1-1, you see Sub Main(). This marks the beginning of the procedure named Main().

This is a special procedure in a Visual Basic program; the Main() procedure is the first procedure that executes when any program runs.

You can tell Main() is a procedure because of the parentheses; all Visual Basic procedure names are followed by parentheses.

6

The programs in the first eight chapters of this book will include only the Main() procedure. In later chapters you will be able to include additional procedures.

The first part of any procedure is its **header**. In Figure 1-1, the header for the Main() procedure begins with the Sub keyword and is followed by the procedure name, which is Main(). The End Sub on the second-to-last line of Figure 1-1 marks the end of the Main() procedure. All the code within the procedure header and the End Sub executes when the Main() procedure executes. In Figure 1-1, there is only this one line of code that executes:

```
System.Console.WriteLine("Hello World.")
```

This is the line that causes the words "Hello World." to appear on the user's screen. This line consists of two parts. The first part, System.Console.WriteLine(), prints (that is, displays on the screen) whatever is included within its parentheses and positions the cursor so any subsequent output appears on the next line. In this example, the parentheses contain the message "Hello World." so that is what will appear on the screen. (The quotation marks will not appear on the screen, but they are necessary to make the program work.)

In the statement System.Console.WriteLine("Hello World."), System is a namespace, Console is an object, and WriteLine() is a method. A **namespace** is a collection of classes. The System namespace includes many of the commonly used classes. Visual Basic programs frequently use the namespace-dot-object-dot-method syntax or the class-dot-object-dot-method syntax.

Next, you learn about the Visual Basic development cycle so that later in this chapter, you can compile the Hello World program and execute it. The Hello World program is saved in a file named HelloWorld.vb and is included in the student files for this chapter.

The Visual Basic Development Cycle

When you finish designing a program and writing the Visual Basic code that implements your design, you must compile and execute your program. This three-step process of writing code, compiling code, and executing code is called the Visual Basic development cycle. It is illustrated in Figure 1-2. Don't be concerned if you don't understand all the terms in Figure 1-2. These terms are explained in the following sections.

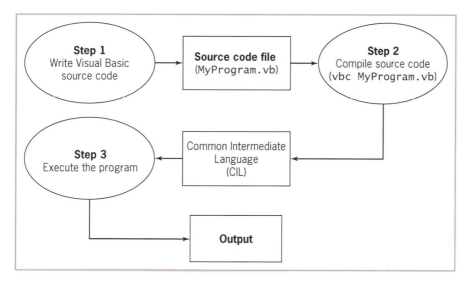

Figure 1-2 The Visual Basic development cycle

Writing Visual Basic Source Code

As you learned in the previous section, you write a Visual Basic program by creating a `Module` and including a procedure named `Main()` in the `Module`. But what do you use to write the program, and where do you save it?

To write a Visual Basic program, you can use any text editor, but the steps in this book assume you are using Windows Notepad. To start Notepad, click the **Start** button, point to **Programs** or **All Programs**, click **Accessories**, and then click **Notepad**. Once Notepad starts, you simply type in your Visual Basic source code. **Source code** is the name used for the statements that make up a Visual Basic program. For example, the code shown in Figure 1-1 is source code.

When you save the file that contains the source code, it is important to add the extension `.vb` to the filename. For the Hello World program, the `Module` is named `HelloWorld`; therefore, it is convenient to name the source code file `HelloWorld.vb`. Of course, it is also important to remember the location of the folder in which you choose to save your source code file.

Compiling a Visual Basic Program

The Visual Basic compiler is named `vbc`, and it is responsible for taking your source code and transforming it into Common Intermediate Language (CIL). **CIL** is intermediate, machine-independent code. **Intermediate** means that the code is between source code and machine code. **Machine code** consists of the 1s and 0s that a computer needs to execute a program. Next, the Visual Basic compiler reads the CIL code and produces an executable file. This file has the same name as the source code file, but it has an `.exe` extension rather than a `.vb` extension.

8

The following steps show how to compile a source code file. These steps assume you have already created and saved the `HelloWorld.vb` source code file.

If you are working in a school computer lab, the PATH environment variable might already have been set for you.

The PATH environment variable tells your operating system which directories on your system contain commands.

1. Set your PATH environment variable. Refer to "Read This Before You Begin" at the front of this book or ask your instructor for instructions on how to set the PATH environment variable.

2. Open a Command Prompt window. To do this in Windows XP, click the **Start** button, point to **All Programs**, point to **Accessories**, and then click **Command Prompt**. In Vista or Windows 7, click the **Start** button, point to **All Programs**, click **Accessories**, and then click **Command Prompt**. The cursor blinks to the right of the current file path.

3. To compile your source code file, you first have to change to the file path containing your source code file. To do this, type **cd driveletter:\path** where **driveletter** is the drive containing your file, and **path** is the path to the folder containing your file. For example, to open a file stored in a folder named "Testing," which is in turn stored in a folder named "My Program," which is stored on the C: drive, you would type **cd c:\My Program\Testing**. After you type the command, press **Enter**. The cursor now blinks next to the file path for the folder containing your source code file.

4. Type the following command, which uses the Visual Basic compiler vbc to compile the program:

    vbc HelloWorld.vb

    If there are no syntax errors in your source code, a file named `HelloWorld.exe` is created, and you will not see anything special happen. If there are syntax errors, you will see error messages on the screen. In that case, you need to go back to Notepad to fix the errors, save the source code file again, and recompile until no syntax errors remain. **Syntax errors** are messages from the compiler that tell you what your errors are and where they are located in your source code file.

5. After the program is compiled, you can use the `dir` command to display a directory listing to see the file named `HelloWorld.exe`. To execute the `dir` command, you type **dir**

at the command prompt. For example, if your source code file is located at C:\My Program\Testing, the command prompt and `dir` command should look like this: **C:\My Program\ Testing> dir**. The `HelloWorld.exe` file should be in the same directory as the source code file, `HelloWorld.vb`.

Step 3 in the development cycle is executing the Visual Basic program. You'll learn about that next.

Executing a Visual Basic Program

As you know, a computer can understand only machine code (1s and 0s). The machine code for your Visual Basic program is stored in a file with an `.exe` extension.

To execute the Hello World program, do the following:

1. Open a Command Prompt window. To do this in Windows XP, click the **Start** button, point to **All Programs**, point to **Accessories**, and then click **Command Prompt**. In Vista or Windows 7, click the **Start** button, point to **All Programs**, click **Accessories**, and then click **Command Prompt**. Change to the file path containing your executable file, if necessary, and then enter the following command:

   HelloWorld

2. When the program executes, the words "Hello World." appear in a Command Prompt window.

Figure 1-3 illustrates the steps involved in compiling `HelloWorld.vb` using the vbc compiler, executing the `dir` command to verify that the file `HelloWorld.exe` was created, and executing the Hello World program.

At this point in your programming career, don't expect to understand the contents of an `.exe` file if you open one using a text editor, such as Notepad.

You must be in the same directory that contains your `.exe` file when you execute the program.

Figure 1-3 Compiling and executing the Hello World program

Exercise 1-1: Understanding How to Compile and Execute Visual Basic Programs

In this exercise, you use what you have learned about compiling and executing Visual Basic programs to answer Questions 1–2.

You have written a Visual Basic program and have stored your source code in a file named MyVBProgram.vb.

1. What command would you use to compile the source code?

   _____

2. What command would you use to execute the program?

   _____

LAB 1.1 Compiling and Executing a Visual Basic Program

In this lab, you compile and execute a prewritten Visual Basic program, and then answer Questions 1–6.

1. Open the source code file named GoodMorning.vb using Notepad or the text editor of your choice.

2. Save this source code file in a directory of your choice, and then change to that directory.

3. Compile the source code file. There should be no syntax errors. Record the command you used to compile the source code file.

   _____

4. Execute the program. Record the command you used to execute the program, and also record the output of this program.

   _____

   _____

5. Modify the program so that it displays "Good Job!," and then change the Module name to GoodJob. Save the file as GoodJob.vb. Compile and execute the program.

6. Modify the Good Job program so that it prints two lines of output. Add a second output statement that displays "Have a great day." Change the Module name to GoodJob2 and then save the modified file as GoodJob2.vb. Compile and execute the program.

CHAPTER 2

Variables, Constants, Operators, and Writing Programs Using Sequential Statements

After studying this chapter, you will be able to:

- ◎ Name variables and use appropriate data types
- ◎ Declare and initialize variables
- ◎ Understand and use unnamed and named constants
- ◎ Use arithmetic operators in expressions
- ◎ Use assignment operators in assignment statements
- ◎ Write Visual Basic comments
- ◎ Write programs using sequential statements and interactive input statements

In this chapter, you learn about writing programs that use variables, constants, and arithmetic operators. You also learn about programs that receive interactive input from a user of your programs. We begin by reviewing variables and constants and learning how to use them in a Visual Basic program. You should do the exercises and labs in this chapter only after you have finished Chapters 2 and 3 of your book, *Programming Logic and Design, Sixth Edition*, by Joyce Farrell.

Variables

As you know, a **variable** is a named location in the computer's memory whose contents can vary (thus the term *variable*). You use variables in a program when you need to store values. The values stored in variables often change as a program executes.

In Visual Basic, it is a good programming practice to declare variables before you use them in a program. Declaring a variable is a two-part process: first, you give the variable a name, and then you specify its data type. You'll learn about data types shortly. But first, we'll focus on the rules for naming variables in Visual Basic.

Variable Names

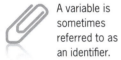

A variable is sometimes referred to as an identifier.

Variable names in Visual Basic can consist of letters, numerical digits, and the underscore character, but they cannot begin with a digit. You should avoid variable names that begin with an underscore because they are not compliant with the **Common Language Specification** (CLS). You will learn more about the CLS in additional courses you take in Visual Basic.

You cannot use a Visual Basic keyword for a variable name. As you learned in Chapter 1 of this book, a keyword is a word with a special meaning in Visual Basic. The following are all examples of legal variable names in Visual Basic: my_var, num6, intValue, and firstName. Table 2-1 lists some examples of invalid variable names, and explains why each is invalid.

Name of Variable	Explanation
3wrong	Invalid because it begins with a digit
don't	Invalid because it contains a single quotation mark
public	Invalid because it is a Visual Basic keyword

Table 2-1   Some examples of invalid variable names

When naming variables, keep in mind that Visual Basic is not **case sensitive**—in other words, Visual Basic does not know the difference between uppercase and lowercase characters. That means `value`, `Value`, and `VaLuE` are the same variable name in Visual Basic.

In Visual Basic, variable names can be 1,023 characters in length. A good rule is to give variables meaningful names that are long enough to describe how the variable is used, but not so long that you make your program hard to read or cause yourself unnecessary typing. For example, a variable named `firstName` will clearly be used to store someone's first name. The variable name `freshmanStudentFirstName` is descriptive but inconveniently long; the variable name `fn` is too short and not meaningful.

One of the naming conventions used by Visual Basic programmers is called **camel case**. This means:

- Variable names are made up of multiple words, with no spaces between them.

- The first character in the variable name is lowercase.

- The first character of each word after the first word is a capitalized character.

Examples of Visual Basic variable names in camel case include `firstName`, `myAge`, and `salePrice`. You do not include spaces between the words in a variable name.

Although Visual Basic is not case sensitive, your programs will be easier for you and other programmers to read if you use uppercase and lowercase characters consistently.

13

Visual Basic Data Types

In addition to specifying a name for a variable, you also need to specify a particular data type for that variable. A variable's **data type** dictates the amount of memory that is allocated for the variable, the type of data that you can store in the variable, and the types of operations that can be performed on the variable. There are many different kinds of data types, but in this book we will focus on the most basic kind of data types, known as **primitive data types**. There are 12 primitive data types in Visual Basic: `Boolean`, `Byte`, `Char`, `Date`, `Double`, `Decimal`, `Integer`, `Long`, `Object`, `Short`, `Single`, and `String`. Some of these data types (`Short`, `Integer`, `Long`, `Double`, and `Single`) are used for variables that store numeric values, and are referred to as numeric data types. The others have specialized purposes. For example, the `Boolean` data type is used to store a value of either `True` or `False`.

You will not use all of Visual Basic's primitive data types in the programs you write in this book. Instead, you will focus on two of the numeric data types (`Integer` and `Double`) and one type that holds text (`String`). The `Integer` data type is used for values that are whole numbers. For example, you could use a variable with the data type `Integer` to store someone's age (for example, 25) or the number of

In *Programming Logic and Design, Sixth Edition,* the data type num is used to refer to all numeric data types. That book does not make a distinction between Integer and Double because the pseudocode used in the book is not specific to any one programming language. However, in Visual Basic this distinction is always maintained.

students in a class (for example, 35). A variable of the Integer data type occupies 32 bits (4 bytes) of space in memory.

You use the data type Double to store a floating point value (that is, a fractional value), such as the price of an item (2.95) or a measurement (2.5 feet). A variable of the Double data type occupies 64 bits (8 bytes) of space in memory. You will learn about using other data types as you continue to learn more about Visual Basic in subsequent courses.

The Integer and Double data types will be adequate for all the numeric variables you will use in this book. But what about when you need to store a group of characters (such as a person's name) in a variable? In programming, we refer to a group of one or more characters as a **string**. An example of a string is the last name "Wallace" or a product type such as a "desk." In Visual Basic, the String primitive data type is used for storing strings.

Exercise 2-1: Using Visual Basic Variables, Data Types, and Keywords

In this exercise, you use what you have learned about naming variables, data types, and keywords to answer Questions 1–2.

1. Is each of the following a legal Visual Basic variable name? (Answer "yes" or "no.")

myAge	_____	this_is_a_var	_____	NUMBER	_____
yourAge	_____	number	_____	$number	_____
Single	_____	1number	_____	intNum	_____
May25	_____	number Two	_____	Number	_____

2. What data type (Integer, Double, or String) is most appropriate for storing each of the following values?

    A person's height (in inches) _____

    The amount of interest on a loan, such as 10% _____

    The price of a pair of boots_____

    The name of your pet _____

    The number of CDs you own _____

Declaring and Initializing Variables

Now that you understand the rules for naming a variable, and you understand the concept of a data type, you are ready to learn how to declare a variable. In Visual Basic, it is a good programming practice to declare all variables before you use them in a program. When you **declare** a variable, you tell the compiler that you are going to use the variable. In the process of declaring a variable, you must specify the variable's name and its data type. Declaring a variable tells the compiler that it needs to reserve a memory location for the variable. A line of code that declares a variable is known as a **variable declaration**. The Visual Basic syntax for a variable declaration is as follows:

```
Dim variableName As dataType
```

For example, the declaration statement `Dim counter As Integer` declares a variable named `counter` of the `Integer` data type. The compiler reserves the amount of memory space allotted to an `Integer` variable (32 bits, or 4 bytes) for the variable named `counter`. The compiler then assigns the new variable a specific memory address. In Figure 2-1, the memory address for the variable named `counter` is 1000, although you wouldn't typically know the memory address of the variables included in your Visual Basic programs.

```
Dim counter As Integer
```

counter (variable name)				another variable
	value of counter			value of the next variable
first byte	second byte	third byte	fourth byte	

1000 (The memory address is assigned by the compiler; you cannot assign the memory address yourself.)

1004 (This is the next available memory address after counter because 4 bytes [1000, 1001, 1002, and 1003] have been reserved for the variable named counter.)

Figure 2-1   Declaration of variable and memory allocation

You can also initialize a Visual Basic variable when you declare it. When you **initialize** a Visual Basic variable, you give it an initial value. For example, you can assign an initial value of 8 to the `counter` variable when you declare it, as shown in the following code:

```
Dim counter As Integer = 8
```

Numeric variables are automatically initialized to zero (0), unless you specify a different value.

You can also declare and initialize variables of data type `Double` and `String` as shown in the following code:

```
Dim salary As Double
Dim cost As Double = 12.95
Dim firstName As String
Dim homeAddress As String = "123 Main Street"
```

Exercise 2-2: Declaring and Initializing Visual Basic Variables

In this exercise, you use what you have learned about declaring and initializing variables to answer Questions 1–2.

1. Write a Visual Basic variable declaration for each of the following. Use Integer, Double, or String and choose meaningful variable names.

    Declare a variable to store a product number (1–1000).

    _____

    Declare a variable to store the number of pets in your family.

    _____

    Declare a variable to store the price of a pair of boots.

    _____

    Declare a variable to store the name of your favorite book.

    _____

2. Declare and initialize variables to represent the following values. Use Integer, Double, or String, and choose meaningful variable names.

    One side of a rectangle that is 5.1 inches in length

    _____

    The number of days in November_____
    The name of your dog, "Duchess"_____
    The number of credit hours you are taking this term

    _____

LAB 2.1   Declaring and Initializing Visual Basic Variables

In this lab, you declare and initialize variables in a Visual Basic program provided with the data files for this book. The program, which is saved in a file named NewAge.vb, calculates your age in the year 2040.

1. Open the source code file named NewAge.vb using Notepad or the text editor of your choice.

2. Declare an integer variable named newAge.

3. Declare and initialize an integer variable named currentAge. Initialize this variable with your current age.

4. Declare and initialize an integer variable named currentYear. Initialize this variable with the value of the current year. Use four digits for the year.

5. Save this source code file in a directory of your choice, and then make that directory your working directory.

6. Compile the source code file NewAge.vb.

7. Execute the program. Record the output of this program.

_____

_____

Constants

As you know, a **constant** is a value that never changes. In Visual Basic, you can use both unnamed constants as well as named constants in a program. You'll learn about named constants shortly. But first, we'll focus on unnamed constants.

Unnamed Constants

Computers are able to deal with two basic types of data: text and numeric. When you use a specific numeric value, such as 35, in a program, you write it using the numbers, without quotation marks. A specific numeric value is called a **numeric constant** because it does not change; a 35 always has the value 35. When you use a specific text value, or string of characters, such as "William," you enclose the **string constant** in double quotation marks. Both of the preceding examples, 35 and "William," are examples of **unnamed constants** because they do not have specified names as variables do.

Named Constants

In addition to variables, Visual Basic allows you to create named constants. A **named constant** is similar to a variable, except it can be assigned a value only once. You use a named constant when you want to assign a name to a value that will never be changed when a program executes.

To declare a named constant in Visual Basic, you use the keyword Const followed by the name of the constant, followed by the keyword As and the data type. Named constants must be initialized when they are declared, and their contents may not be changed during the execution of the program. For example, the following statement declares an Integer constant named MAX_STUDENTS and initializes MAX_STUDENTS with the value 35.

```
Const MAX_STUDENTS As Integer = 35
```

 By convention, in Visual Basic the names of constants are written in all uppercase letters. This makes it easier for you to spot named constants in a long block of code.

Exercise 2-3: Declaring and Initializing Visual Basic Constants

In this exercise, you use what you have learned about declaring and initializing constants to answer the following question.

1. Declare and initialize constants to represent the following values. Use Integer, Double, or String and choose meaningful names.

    The price of a car wash is $14.95._____

    The number of days in November is 30._____

    The name of your dog is "Duchess"._____

    The maximum number of credit hours you may take in a term is 18._____

LAB 2.2 Declaring and Initializing Visual Basic Constants

In this lab, you declare and initialize constants in a Visual Basic program provided with the data files for this book. The program, which is saved in a file named NewAge2.vb, calculates your age in the year 2040.

1. Open the source code file named NewAge2.vb using Notepad or the text editor of your choice.

2. Declare a constant named YEAR and initialize YEAR with the value 2040.

3. Edit the following statement so that it uses the constant named YEAR:

    ```
    newAge = currentAge + (2040 - currentYear)
    ```

4. Edit the following statement, so that it uses the constant named YEAR:

    ```
    System.Console.WriteLine ("I'll be" & newAge & "in 2040.")
    ```

5. Save this source code file as NewAge2.vb in a directory of your choice, and then make that directory your working directory.

6. Compile the source code file NewAge2.vb.

7. Execute the program. Record the output of this program.

    _____

    _____

Arithmetic and Assignment Operators

After you declare a variable, you can use it in various tasks. For example, you can use variables in simple arithmetic calculations, such as adding, subtracting, and multiplying. You can also perform other kinds of operations with variables, such as comparing one variable to another to determine which is greater.

In order to write Visual Basic code that manipulates variables in this way, you need to be familiar with operators. An **operator** is a symbol that tells the computer to perform a mathematical or logical operation. Visual Basic has a large assortment of operators. We begin the discussion with a group of operators known as the arithmetic operators.

Arithmetic Operators

Arithmetic operators are the symbols used to perform arithmetic calculations. You are probably already very familiar with the arithmetic operators for addition (+) and subtraction (-). Table 2-2 lists and explains Visual Basic's arithmetic operators.

Operator Name and Symbol	Example	Comment
Addition +	`num1 + num2`	
Subtraction –	`num1 - num2`	
Multiplication *	`num1 * num2`	
Integer Division \	`15\2`	Integer division; result is 7; fraction is truncated
Division /	`15/2`	Floating-point division; result is 7.5
	`15.0 / 2.0`	Floating-point division; result is 7.5
	`15.0 / 2`	Floating-point division; result is 7.5
Modulus MOD	`hours MOD 24`	Performs division and finds the remainder; result is 1 if the value of `hours` is 25
Negation –	`-(num1 - num2)`	If value of (`num1 - num2`) is 10, then `-(num1 - num2)` is −10
Exponentiation ^	`2 ^ 3`	Raises 2 to the third power; result is 8

Table 2-2   Visual Basic arithmetic operators

You can combine arithmetic operators and variables to create **expressions**. The computer evaluates each expression, and the result is a value. To give you an idea of how this works, assume that the value of `num1` is 3 and `num2` is 20, and that both are data type `Integer`.

With this information in mind, study the examples of expressions and their values in Table 2-3.

Expression	Value	Explanation
num1 + num2	23	3 + 20 = 23
num1 - num 2	–17	3 – 20 = –17
num2 MOD num1	2	20 / 3 = 6 remainder 2
num1 * num2	60	3 * 20 = 60
num2 / num1	6.66666	20 / 3 = 6.66666 (floating point division)
num2 \ num1	6	20 / 3 = 6 (remainder is truncated)
-num1	–3	Value of num1 is 3, therefore -num1 is –3
num2 ^ num1	8000	20 raised to the third power is 8000

Table 2-3   Expressions and values

Assignment Operators and the Assignment Statement

Another type of operator is an **assignment operator**. You use an assignment operator to assign a value to a variable. A statement that assigns a value to a variable is known as an **assignment statement**. In Visual Basic, there are several types of assignment operators. The one you will use most often is the = assignment operator, which simply assigns a value to a variable. Table 2-4 lists and explains some of Visual Basic's assignment operators.

Operator Name and Symbol	Example	Comment
Assignment =	count = 5	Places the value on the right side into the memory location named on the left side
Initialization =	Dim count As Integer = 5	Places the value on the right side into the memory location named on the left side when the variable is declared
Assignment +=	num += 20	Equivalent to num = num + 20
Assignment -=	num -= 20	Equivalent to num = num - 20
Assignment *=	num *= 20	Equivalent to num = num * 20
Assignment /=	num /= 20	Equivalent to num = num / 20
Assignment \=	num \= 20	Equivalent to num = num \ 20
Assignment ^=	num ^= 20	Equivalent to num = num ^ 20

Table 2-4   Visual Basic assignment operators

When an assignment statement executes, the computer evaluates the expression on the right side of the assignment operator and then assigns the result to the memory location associated with the variable named on the left side of the assignment operator. An example of an assignment statement is shown in the following code:

```
answer = num1 * num2
```

This assignment statement causes the computer to evaluate the expression num1 * num2. After evaluating the expression, the computer stores the result in the memory location associated with answer. If the value stored in the variable named num1 is 3, and the value stored in the variable named num2 is 20, then the value 60 is assigned to the variable named answer.

Here is another example:

```
answer += num1
```

This statement is equivalent to the following statement:

```
answer = answer + num1
```

If the value of answer is currently 10 and the value of num1 is 3, then the expression on the right side of the assignment statement answer + num1 evaluates to 13, and the computer assigns the value 13 to answer.

Precedence and Associativity

Once you start to write code that includes operators, you need to be aware of the order in which a series of operations is performed. In other words, you need to be aware of the **precedence** of operations in your code. Each operator is assigned a certain level of precedence. For example, multiplication has a higher level of precedence than addition. So in the expression 3 * 7 + 2, the 3 * 7 would be multiplied first; after the multiplication is completed, the 2 is added.

But what happens when two operators have the same precedence? The rules of **associativity** determine the order in which operations are evaluated in an expression containing two or more operators with the same precedence. For example, in the expression 3 + 7 - 2, the addition and subtraction operators have the same precedence. As shown in Table 2-5, the addition and subtraction operators have left-to-right associativity, which causes the expression to be evaluated from left to right (3 + 7 added first; then 2 is subtracted). Table 2-5 shows the precedence and associativity of the operators discussed in this chapter.

Operator Name	Operator Symbol	Order of Precedence	Associativity
Parentheses	( )	First	Left to right
Exponentiation	^	Second	Left to right
Negation	–	Third	Right to left
Multiplication and division	* /	Fourth	Left to right
Integer division	\	Fifth	Left to right
Modulus	MOD	Sixth	Left to right
Addition and subtraction	+ -	Seventh	Left to right
Assignment	= += -= *= /= \= ^=	Eighth	Right to left

Table 2-5   Order of precedence and associativity

As you can see in Table 2-5, the parentheses operator ( ) has the highest precedence. You use this operator to change the order in which operations are performed. Note the following example:

```
average = test1 + test2 / 2
```

The task of this statement is to find the average of two test scores. The way this statement is currently written, the compiler will divide the value in the test2 variable by 2, and then add it to the value in the test1 variable. So, for example, if the value of test1 is 90 and the value of test2 is 88, then the value assigned to average will be 134, which is obviously not the correct average of these two test scores. By using the parentheses operator in this example, you can force the addition to occur before the division. The correct statement looks like this:

```
average = (test1 + test2) / 2
```

In this example, the value of test1, 90, is added to the value of test2, 88, and then the sum is divided by 2. The value assigned to average, 89, is the correct result.

Exercise 2-4: Understanding Operator Precedence and Associativity

In this exercise, you use what you have learned about operator precedence and associativity. Study the following code and then answer Questions 1–2.

```
' This program demonstrates the precedence and
' associativity of operators.
Module Operators
    Sub Main()
        Dim value1 As Integer = 8
        Dim value2 As Integer = 2
        Dim value3 As Integer = 11
        Dim answer1 As Integer
        Dim answer2 As Integer
        Dim answer3 As Integer
        Dim answer4 As Integer
        Dim answer5 As Integer
        Dim answer6 As Integer

        answer1 = value1 * value2 + value3
        System.Console.WriteLine("Answer 1: " & answer1)

        answer2 = value1 * (value2 + value3)
        System.Console.WriteLine("Answer 2: " & answer2)

        answer3 = value1 + value2 - value3
        System.Console.WriteLine("Answer 3: " & answer3)

        answer4 = value1 + (value2 - value3)
        System.Console.WriteLine("Answer 4: " & answer4)

        answer5 = value1 + value2 * value3
        System.Console.WriteLine("Answer 5: " & answer5)

        answer6 = value3 / value2
        System.Console.WriteLine("Answer 6: " & answer6)

    End Sub
End Module
```

1. What is the value of answer1, answer2, answer3, answer4, answer5, and answer6?

    _____

2. Explain how precedence and associativity affect the result.

    _____
    _____
    _____
    _____
    _____
    _____

LAB 2.3   Arithmetic and Assignment Operators

In this lab, you complete a Visual Basic program that is provided along with the data files for this book. The program, which was written for an appliance company, prints the name of an appliance, its retail price, its wholesale price, the profit made on the appliance, a sale price, and the profit made when the sale price is used.

1. Open the file named `Appliance.vb` using Notepad or the text editor of your choice.

2. The file includes variable declarations and output statements. Read them carefully before you proceed to the next step.

3. Design the logic and write the Visual Basic code that will use assignment statements to first calculate the profit, then calculate the sale price, and finally calculate the profit when the sale price is used. Profit is defined as the retail price minus the wholesale price. The sale price is 20% deducted from the retail price. The sale profit is defined as the sale price minus the wholesale price. Perform the appropriate calculations as part of your assignment statements.

4. Save the source code file in a directory of your choice, and then make that directory your working directory.

5. Compile the program.

6. Execute the program. Your output should be as follows:

   • Item Name: Dishwasher

   • Retail Price: $425

   • Wholesale Price: $275

   • Profit: $150

   • Sale Price: $340

   • Sale Profit: $65

Next, you see how to put together all you have learned in this chapter to write a Visual Basic program that uses sequential statements, comments, and interactive input statements.

Sequential Statements, Comments, and Interactive Input Statements

The term **sequential statements** (or **sequence**), refers to a series of statements that must be performed in sequential order, one after another. You use a sequence in programs when you want to perform actions one after the other. A sequence can contain any number of actions, but those actions must be in the proper order, and no action in the sequence can be skipped. Note that a sequence can contain comments that are not considered part of the sequence itself.

Comments serve as documentation, explaining the code to the programmer and any other people who might read it. In Chapter 2 of *Programming Logic and Design, Sixth Edition*, you learned about program comments, which are statements that do not execute. You use comments in Visual Basic programs to explain your logic to people who read your source code. The Visual Basic compiler ignores comments.

In Visual Basic, you type an apostrophe character (') at the beginning of the text that you want the compiler to ignore. You may place comments anywhere in a Visual Basic program. In the Visual Basic program below, the first five lines of the program are comments that explain some basic information about the program. Comments are included throughout to describe various parts of the program.

A sequence often includes **interactive input statements**, which are statements that ask, or **prompt**, the user to input data. The Visual Basic program in the following example uses sequential statements and interactive input statements to convert a Fahrenheit temperature to its Celsius equivalent:

You are responsible for including well-written, meaningful comments in all of the programs that you write. In fact, some people think that commenting your source code is as important as the source code itself.

```
' This Visual Basic program converts a Fahrenheit
' temperature to Celsius.
' Input: Interactive
' Output: Fahrenheit temperature followed by
' Celsius temperature
Option Explicit On
Option Strict On
Module Temperature
   Sub Main()
      Dim fahrenheitString As String
      Dim fahrenheit As Double
      Dim celsius As Double
      ' Get interactive user input
      fahrenheitString = InputBox$( _
           "Enter Fahrenheit temperature: ")
      ' Convert String to Double
      fahrenheit = Convert.ToDouble(fahrenheitString)
      ' Calculate celsius
      celsius = (fahrenheit - 32.0) * (5.0/9.0)
      ' Output
      System.Console.WriteLine("Fahrenheit temperature:" & _
                          fahrenheit)
      System.Console.WriteLine("Celsius temperature:" & _
                          celsius)
   End Sub
End Module
```

This program is made up of sequential statements that execute one after the other. As noted above, it also includes comments explaining the code. The comment lines begin with '.

The statement, `Option Explicit On`, turns on the Visual Basic option that requires you to declare all variables in your program. The default in Visual Basic is that this option is on. The statement, `Option Strict On`, turns on the Visual Basic option that requires you to declare variables with a specific type and can therefore accept only values of that data type. The `Strict` option must be turned on to enforce **strong typing**. The `Strict` option is turned off by default. It is highly recommended that you turn on this option; you should get in the habit of including this statement in all your Visual Basic programs.

After the variable `fahrenheitString` is declared as a `String`, and `fahrenheit` and `celsius` are declared (using the `Double` data type), the following assignment statement executes:

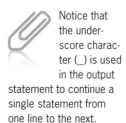

Notice that the under-score charac-ter (_) is used in the output statement to continue a single statement from one line to the next.

```
fahrenheitString = InputBox$( _
    "Enter Fahrenheit temperature:")
```

The `InputBox$()` function (on the right side of the assignment statement) is used when you want the program's user to interactively input data needed by your program. When you use the `InputBox$()` function, you specify within the parentheses the words you want to appear in the dialog box on the user's screen. In this example, the phrase "Enter Fahrenheit temperature:" will appear in the dialog box on the user's screen. The same dialog box also displays a text box where the user can type his or her input, as shown in Figure 2-2.

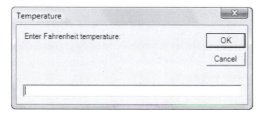

Figure 2-2   An input dialog box

In this program, you want the user to input a Fahrenheit temperature value so that the program can convert it to Celsius. You would think, then, that this would be a simple matter of taking the value entered by the user, assigning it to a variable, and then performing the necessary conversion calculation. However, Visual Basic considers any input entered into an input dialog box to be a string. In this case, the Fahrenheit value input by the user is assigned to the `String` variable named `fahrenheitString`. The problem is that we can't perform calculations on strings; we can only perform calculations on numeric variables. So, before the program can proceed with the calculation required to convert a Fahrenheit value to a Celsius value, we need to transfer the value entered by the user to a variable with a numeric data type.

That task is performed by the following assignment statement, which is the second statement to execute:

```
fahrenheit = Convert.ToDouble(fahrenheitString)
```

The ToDouble() method is used on the right side of this assignment statement. This method belongs to the Convert class and is used to convert the Fahrenheit value, which the compiler automatically considered a String, to the Double data type. Once the String is converted to Double, it is assigned to the variable fahrenheit (which, at the beginning of the program, was declared as a Double).

The third statement to execute is another assignment statement, as follows:

```
celsius = (fahrenheit - 32.0) * (5.0 / 9.0)
```

The formula that converts Fahrenheit temperatures to Celsius is used on the right side of this assignment statement. Notice the use of parentheses in the expression to control precedence. The expression is evaluated, and the resulting value is assigned to the variable named celsius.

Notice that the division uses the / operator. This is an example of floating-point division, which results in a value that includes a fraction. If the \ operator were used, integer division would be performed, and the fractional portion would be truncated. This would result in a value of 0.

The next two statements to execute in sequence are both output statements, as follows:

```
System.Console.WriteLine("Fahrenheit temperature:" & _
                         fahrenheit)
System.Console.WriteLine("Celsius temperature:" & _
                         celsius)
```

The statement System.Console.WriteLine() is used to output whatever is within the parentheses. The first output statement displays the words "Fahrenheit temperature:" followed by the value stored in the variable fahrenheit. The second output statement displays the words "Celsius temperature:" followed by the value stored in the variable celsius. To use the WriteLine() method correctly, you include only one argument within the parentheses. Arguments are discussed briefly in Chapter 3 and in more detail in Chapter 9. The concatenation operator is used in both output statements to combine two items into one (a **string constant**, which is one or more characters within

In *Program-*
ming Logic
and Design,
Sixth Edition,
the comma
(,) is used as the concatenation operator.

28

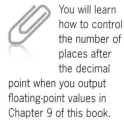

You will learn
how to control
the number of
places after
the decimal
point when you output
floating-point values in
Chapter 9 of this book.

double quotes, and a `Double`). The & symbol, when used in this con-
text, is the **concatenation** operator. It is used to combine two values
next to each other to create a single string.

This program is saved in a file named `Temperature.vb` and is
included in the student files for this chapter. You can see the output
produced by the Temperature program in Figure 2-3.

Figure 2-3   Output produced by the `Temperature.vb` program

Now that you have seen a complete Visual Basic program that uses
sequential statements and interactive input statements, it is time for
you to begin writing your own programs.

Exercise 2-5: Understanding Sequential Statements

In this exercise, you use what you have learned about sequential statements. Read the following scenario and then answer Questions 1–4.

Suppose you have written a Visual Basic program that calculates the
amount of paint you need to cover the walls in your family room.
Two walls are 10 feet high and 18.5 feet wide. The other two walls are
10 feet high and 20.5 feet wide. The salesperson at the home improve-
ment store told you to buy 1 gallon of paint for every 150 square feet
of wall you need to paint. Suppose you wrote the following code, but
your program is not compiling. This program is saved in a file named
`Paint.vb` and is included in the student files for this chapter. Take a
few minutes to study this code and then answer Questions 1–4.

```
' This program calculates the number of gallons
' of paint needed.
Option Explicit On
Option Strict On
Module Paint
    Sub Main()
        Dim height1 As Double = 10
        Dim height2 As Double = 10
        Dim width1 As Integer = 18.5
        Dim width2 As Double = 20.5
        Dim squareFeet As Double
        Dim numGallons As Integer
```

```
      numGallons = squareFeet / 150
      squareFeet = (width1 * height1 + width2 * height2) * 2
      System.Console.WriteLine("Number of Gallons:" & _
                          numGallons)
   End Sub
End Module
```

1. The first error is in this line of code.

   ```
   Dim width1 As Integer = 18.5
   ```

   What do you have to do to fix this problem? _____

2. The second error has to do with these three lines of code.

   ```
   Dim squareFeet As Double
   Dim numGallons As Integer

   numGallons = squareFeet / 150
   ```

   What must you do to fix this problem? _____

3. Even if you fix the problems identified in Question 1 and Question 2, you still have a problem with this program. It has to do with the order in which your statements are written. Identify the problem, and then determine what you need to do to fix the problem. On the following lines, describe how to fix the problem.

   _____
   _____
   _____

4. You have two variables declared in this program to represent the height of your walls, height1 and height2. Do you need both of these variables? If not, how would you change the program? Be sure to identify all of the changes you would make.

   _____
   _____
   _____
   _____
   _____

LAB 2.4 Using Sequential Statements in a Visual Basic Program

In this lab, you complete a Visual Basic program provided with the data files for this book. The program calculates the amount of tax withheld from an employee's weekly salary, the tax deduction to which the employee is entitled for each dependent, and the employee's take-home pay. The program output includes state tax withheld, federal tax withheld, dependent tax deductions, salary, and take-home pay.

1. Open the source code file named `Payroll.vb` using Notepad or the text editor of your choice.

2. Variables have been declared and initialized for you as needed, and the output statements have been written. Read the code carefully before you proceed to the next step.

3. Write the Visual Basic code needed to perform the following:

   • Calculate state withholding tax at 3.0%, and calculate federal withholding tax at 30.0%.

   • Calculate dependent deductions at 5.0% of the employee's salary for each dependent.

   • Calculate total withholding.

   • Calculate take-home pay as salary minus total withholding plus deductions.

4. Save this source code file in a directory of your choice, and then make that directory your working directory.

5. Compile the program.

6. Execute the program. You should get the following output:

   • State Tax: $28.5

   • Federal Tax: $285

   • Dependents: $142.5

   • Salary: $950

   • Take-Home Pay: $779

7. In this program, the variables named `salary` and `numDependents` are initialized with the values 950.0 and 3. To make this program more flexible, modify it to accept interactive input for `salary` and `numDependents`. Name the modified version `Payroll2.vb`.

CHAPTER 3

Writing Structured Visual Basic Programs

After studying this chapter, you will be able to:

◎ Use structured flowcharts and pseudocode to write structured Visual Basic programs

◎ Write simple modular programs in Visual Basic

In this chapter, you begin to learn how to write structured Visual Basic programs. As you will see, creating a flowchart and writing pseudocode before you actually write the program ensures that you fully understand the program's intended design. We begin by looking at a structured flowchart and pseudocode from your text, *Programming Logic and Design, Sixth Edition*. You should do the exercises and labs in this chapter only after you have finished Chapters 2 and 3 of that book.

Using Flowcharts and Pseudocode to Write a Visual Basic Program

In the first three chapters of *Programming Logic and Design, Sixth Edition*, you studied flowcharts and pseudocode for the Number-Doubling program. Figure 3-1 shows the functional, structured flowchart and pseudocode for this program.

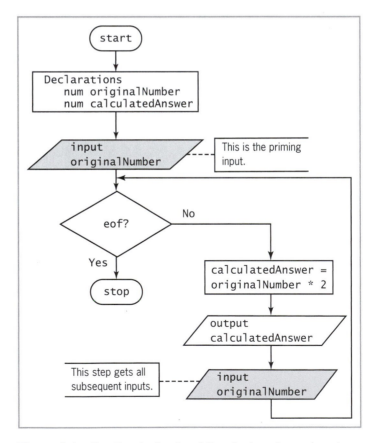

Figure 3-1 Functional, structured flowchart, and pseudocode for the Number-Doubling program

By studying the flowchart and pseudocode, you can see that this program makes use of the sequence and loop structures introduced to you in *Programming Logic and Design, Sixth Edition*. The remainder of this section walks you through the Visual Basic code for this program. The explanations assume that you are simply reading along, but if you want, you can type the code as it is presented. The goal of this section is to help you get a feel for how flowcharts and pseudocode can serve as a guide as you write Visual Basic programs. You must learn more about Visual Basic before you can expect to write this program by yourself.

In Figure 3-1, the first line of the pseudocode is the word `start`. How do we translate this pseudocode command into the Visual Basic code that will start the Number-Doubling program? In Chapter 1 of this book, you learned that, to start a Visual Basic program, you first create a `Module`. So, to start the Number-Doubling program, we will first create a module named `NumberDouble`. We should also include one procedure in the module named `Main()`, which is always the first procedure that executes in a Visual Basic program. Thus, the code that follows starts the Number-Doubling program by including the statements that turn on the `Explicit` and `Strict` options, creating a module named `NumberDouble` and including the `Main()` procedure:

```
Option Explicit On
Option Strict On
Module NumberDouble
    Sub Main()
    End Sub
End Module
```

Next, you see that two variables, `originalNumber` and `calculatedAnswer`, are declared as data type `num`. The Visual Basic code that follows adds the variable declarations, with the declarations shown in bold.

```
Option Explicit On
Option Strict On
Module NumberDouble
    Sub Main()
        Dim originalNumber As Integer
        Dim calculatedAnswer As Integer
    End Sub
End Module
```

The next line of the pseudocode instructs you to input the `originalNumber`. In other words, you need to write the input statement that primes the loop. You learned about priming read statements in Chapter 3 of *Programming Logic and Design, Sixth Edition*. In Chapter 2 of this book, you learned how to use interactive input statements in programs to allow the user to input data. You

If you are typing the code as it is presented here, save the program in a file that has an appropriate name, such as `NumberDouble.vb`. The complete program is also saved in a file named `NumberDouble.vb` and is included in the student files for this chapter.

also learned to prompt the user by explaining what the program expects to receive as input. The following example includes the code that implements the priming read by displaying a dialog box where users can input the number they want doubled. The next statement converts the input String to an Integer.

The code in boldface has been added to the NumberDouble module in the Main() procedure. The String variable named originalNumberString is added to hold the input entered into the input dialog box. If you were writing this code yourself, you would start by writing the code for the NumberDouble module, and then edit it to add the boldface code shown here:

```
Option Explicit On
Option Strict On
Module NumberDouble
    Sub Main()
        Dim originalNumber As Integer
        Dim originalNumberString As String
        Dim calculatedAnswer As Integer
        originalNumberString = InputBox$( _
                    "Enter number to double : ")
        originalNumber = Convert.ToInt32(originalNumberString)
    End Sub
End Module
```

You have not learned enough about while loops to write this code yourself, but you can observe how it is done in this example. You will learn more about loops in Chapter 5 of this book.

Next, the pseudocode instructs you to begin a while loop with eof (end of file) used as the condition to exit the loop.

Since we are using interactive input in this program, it requires no eof marker. Instead we will use the number 0 (zero) to indicate the end of input. We'll use 0 because 0 doubled will always be 0. The use of 0 to indicate the end of input also requires us to change the prompt to tell the user how to end the program. Review the following code. Again, the newly added code is formatted in bold.

```
Option Explicit On
Option Strict On
Module NumberDouble
    Sub Main()
        Dim originalNumber As Integer
        Dim originalNumberString As String
        Dim calculatedAnswer As Integer
        originalNumberString = InputBox$( _
                    "Enter number to double " & _
                    " or 0 to end: ")
        originalNumber = Convert.ToInt32(originalNumberString)
        While originalNumber <> 0
        End While
    End Sub
End Module
```

According to the pseudocode, the body of the loop is made up of three sequential statements. The first statement calculates the originalNumber multiplied by 2; the second statement prints the calculatedAnswer; and the third statement retrieves the next originalNumber from the user. In Visual Basic, we actually need to add an additional, fourth statement in the body of the While loop. This fourth statement converts the input String to an Integer.

In the following example, the code that makes up the body of the loop is in bold.

```
Option Explicit On
Option Strict On
Module NumberDouble
    Sub Main()
        Dim originalNumber As Integer
        Dim originalNumberString As String
        Dim calculatedAnswer As Integer
        originalNumberString = InputBox$( _
                    "Enter number to double " & _
                    " or 0 to end: ")
        originalNumber = Convert.ToInt32(originalNumberString)
        While originalNumber <> 0
            calculatedAnswer = originalNumber * 2
            System.Console.WriteLine(originalNumber & _
                        " doubled is " & calculatedAnswer)
            originalNumberString = InputBox$( _
                        "Enter number to double " & _
                        "or 0 to end: ")
            originalNumber = Convert.ToInt32( _
                        originalNumberString)
        End While
    End Sub
End Module
```

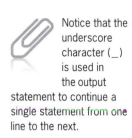

Notice that the underscore character (_) is used in the output statement to continue a single statement from one line to the next.

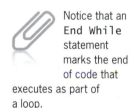

Notice that an End While statement marks the end of code that executes as part of a loop.

The last line of the pseudocode instructs you to end the program. In Visual Basic, the End Sub statement signifies the end of the Main() procedure, and the End Module statement ends the NumberDouble module.

At this point, the program is ready to be compiled. Assuming there are no syntax errors, it should execute as planned. Figure 3-2 displays the input and output of the Number Double program.

36

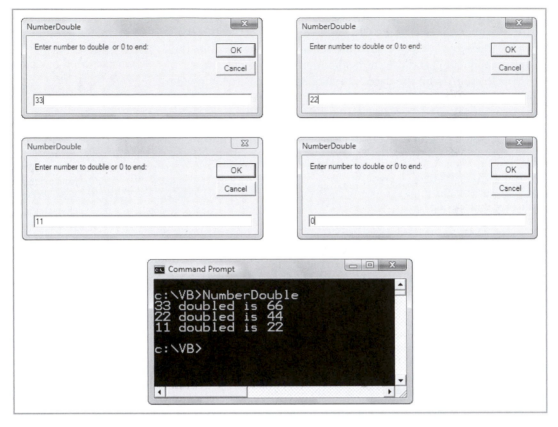

Figure 3-2 Number Double program input and output

Although you have not learned everything you need to know to write this program yourself, you can see from this example that writing the program in Visual Basic is easier if you start with a well-designed, functional, structured flowchart or pseudocode.

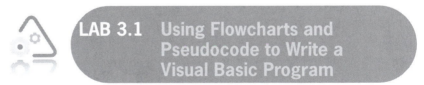

LAB 3.1 Using Flowcharts and Pseudocode to Write a Visual Basic Program

In this lab, you use the pseudocode in Figure 3-3 to add code to a partially created Visual Basic program. When completed, college admissions officers should be able to use the Visual Basic program to determine whether to accept or reject a student, based on his or her test score and class rank.

```
start
    input testScore, classRank
    if testScore >= 90 then
        if classRank >= 25 then
            output "Accept"
        else
            output "Reject"
        endif
    else
        if testScore >= 80 then
            if classRank >= 50 then
                output "Accept"
            else
                output "Reject"
            endif
        else
            if testScore >= 70 then
                if classRank >= 75 then
                    output "Accept"
                else
                    output "Reject"
                endif
            else
                output "Reject"
            endif
        endif
    endif
stop
```

Figure 3-3   Pseudocode for the College Admission program

1. Study the pseudocode in Figure 3-3.

2. Open the source code file named CollegeAdmission.vb using Notepad or the text editor of your choice.

3. Declare two String variables named testScoreString and classRankString.

4. Declare two Integer variables named testScore and classRank.

5. Write the interactive input statements to retrieve a student's test score and class rank from the user of the program.

6. Write the statements to convert the String representation of a student's test score and class rank to the Integer data type.

7. The rest of the program is written for you. Save this source code file in a directory of your choice, and then make that directory your working directory.

8. Compile the source code file `CollegeAdmission.vb`.

9. Execute the program by entering 30 for the test score and 95 for the class rank. Record the output of this program.

_____

10. Execute the program by entering 95 for the test score and 30 for the class rank. Record the output of this program.

_____

Writing a Modular Program in Visual Basic

In Chapter 2 of your book, *Programming Logic and Design, Sixth Edition*, you learned about local and global variables and named constants. To review briefly, you declare **local variables** and local constants within the procedure that uses them. Further, you can only use a local variable or a local constant within the procedure in which it is declared. **Global variables** and global constants are known to the entire program. They are declared at the program level and are visible to and usable in all the procedures called by the program. It is not considered a good programming practice to use global variables, so the Visual Basic program below uses local variables (as well as local constants). A good reason for using local variables and local constants is that source code is easier to understand when variables are declared where they are used. In addition, global variables can be accessed and altered by any part of the program, which can make the program difficult to read and maintain and also prone to error.

Recall from Chapter 2 that most programs consist of a main module or procedure that contains the mainline logic. The mainline logic of most procedural programs follows this general structure:

1. Declarations of variables and constants

2. **Housekeeping tasks**, such as displaying instructions to users, displaying report headings, opening files the program requires, and inputting the first data item

3. **Detail loop tasks** that do the main work of the program, such as processing many records and performing calculations

4. **End-of-job tasks**, such as displaying totals and closing any open files

In Chapter 2 of *Programming Logic and Design, Sixth Edition,* you studied a flowchart and pseudocode for a modular program that prints a payroll report with global variables and constants. This flowchart and pseudocode are shown in Figure 3-4.

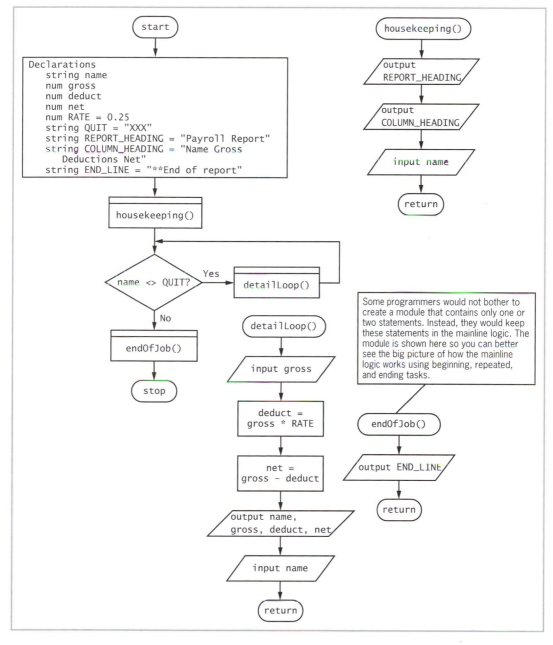

Figure 3-4 Flowchart and pseudocode for the Payroll Report program *(continues)*

(continued)

40

```
start
   Declarations
      string name
      num gross
      num deduct
      num net
      num RATE = 0.25
      string QUIT = "XXX"
      string REPORT_HEADING = "Payroll Report"
      string COLUMN_HEADING = "Name  Gross  Deductions  Net"
      string END_LINE = "**End of report"
   housekeeping()
   while not name = QUIT
      detailLoop()
   endwhile
   endOfJob()
stop

housekeeping()
   output REPORT_HEADING
   output COLUMN_HEADING
   input name
return

detailLoop()
   input gross
   deduct = gross * RATE
   net = gross - deduct
   output name, gross, deduct, net
   input name
return

endOfJob()
   output END_LINE
return
```

Figure 3-4   Flowchart and pseudocode for the Payroll Report program

In this section, we walk through the process of creating a Visual Basic program that implements the logic illustrated in the flowchart in Figure 3-4. According to the flowchart, the program begins with the execution of the mainline method. The mainline method in the flowchart declares four global variables (name, gross, deduct, and net) and five global constants (RATE, QUIT, REPORT_HEADING, COLUMN_HEADING, and END_LINE).

The Visual Basic code that follows shows the creation of the `PayrollReport` module, the `Main()` procedure, and variable and constant declarations.

```
Option Explicit On
Option Strict On
Module PayrollReport
    Sub Main()
        Dim name As String
        Dim grossString As String
        Dim gross, deduct, net As Double
        Const RATE As Double = 0.25
        Const QUIT As String = "XXX"
        Const REPORT_HEADING As String = "Payroll Report"
        Const END_LINE As String = "**End of report"
    End Sub
End Module
```

If you are typing the code as it is presented here, save the program in a file that is named appropriately, for example, `PayrollReport.vb`. The complete program is also saved in a file named `PayrollReport.vb` and is included in the student files for this chapter.

41

Notice that one of the declarations shown in the flowchart, `String COLUMN_HEADING = "Name Gross Deductions Net,"` is not included in the Visual Basic code. Since you have not yet learned about the Visual Basic statements needed to line up values in report format, the Visual Basic program shown above prints information on separate lines rather than in the column format used in the flowchart. Also, notice that the Visual Basic code includes one additional variable, `grossString`, which is used to hold the user-entered value for an employee's gross pay. Later in the program, the `String` variable, `grossString`, is converted to a `Double` so that it may be used in calculations.

It is important for you to understand that the variables and constants declared in the flowchart are global variables that may be used in all modules that are part of the program. However, as mentioned earlier, it is not considered good programming practice to use global variables. The variables and constants declared in the Visual Basic version are local, which means they may only be used in the `Main()` procedure.

By convention, in Visual Basic the names of constants appear in camel case or in all uppercase. Some programmers believe using all uppercase makes it easier for you to spot named constants in a long block of code.

After the declarations, the flowchart makes a call to the `housekeeping()` module that prints the `REPORT_HEADING` and `COLUMN_HEADING` constants and retrieves the first employee's name that is entered by the user of the program. The code that follows shows how these tasks are translated to Visual Basic statements. The added code is shown in bold.

```
Option Explicit On
Option Strict On
Module PayrollReport
    Sub Main()
        Dim name As String
        Dim grossString As String
        Dim gross, deduct, net As Double
        Const RATE As Double = 0.25
        Const QUIT As String = "XXX"
        Const REPORT_HEADING As String = "Payroll Report"
        Const END_LINE As String = "**End of report"

        ' Work done in the housekeeping() procedure
        System.Console.WriteLine(REPORT_HEADING)
        name = InputBox$("Enter employee's name: ")
    End Sub
End Module
```

Since it is not considered good programming practice to use global variables, all of the variables and constants declared for this program are local and are available only in the Main() procedure. If we were to create an additional procedure for the housekeeping tasks, that procedure would not have access to the name variable to store an employee's name. So, for now, the Visual Basic programs that you write will have only one procedure (module), the Main() procedure. Additional modules, such as the housekeeping() module, will be simulated through the use of comments. As shown in the preceding code, the statements that would execute as part of a housekeeping() procedure have been grouped together in the Visual Basic program and preceded by a comment. You will learn how to create additional procedures and pass data to procedures in Chapter 9 of this book.

In the flowchart, the next statement to execute after the housekeeping() module finishes its work is a while loop in the main module that continues to execute until the user enters "XXX" when prompted for an employee's name. Within the loop, the detailLoop() module is called. The work done in the detailLoop() consists of retrieving an employee's gross pay; calculating deductions; calculating net pay; printing the employee's name, gross pay, deductions, and net pay on the user's screen; and retrieving the name of the next employee. The following code shows the Visual Basic statements that have been added to the Payroll Report program to implement this logic. The added statements are shown in bold.

```
Option Explicit On
Option Strict On
Module PayrollReport
    Sub Main()
        Dim name As String
        Dim grossString As String
        Dim gross, deduct, net As Double
        Const RATE As Double = 0.25
        Const QUIT As String = "XXX"
        Const REPORT_HEADING As String = "Payroll Report"
        Const END_LINE As String = "**End of report"

        ' Work done in the housekeeping() procedure
        System.Console.WriteLine(REPORT_HEADING)
        name = InputBox$("Enter employee's name: ")
        While(name <> QUIT)
            ' Work done in the detailLoop() procedure
            grossString = InputBox$( _
                            "Enter employee's gross pay: ")
            gross = Convert.ToDouble(grossString)
            deduct = gross * RATE
            net = gross - deduct
            System.Console.WriteLine("Name: " & name)
            System.Console.WriteLine ("Gross Pay: " & gross)
            System.Console.WriteLine ("Deductions: " & deduct)
            System.Console.WriteLine ("Net Pay: " & net)
            name = InputBox$("Enter employee's name: ")
        End While
    End Sub
End Module
```

The While loop in the Visual Basic program compares the name entered by the user with the value of the constant named QUIT. As long as the name is not equal to "XXX" (the value of QUIT), the loop executes. The statements that make up the simulated detailLoop() method include: retrieving the employee's gross pay; converting the grossString value to a Double using the Convert.ToDouble() method; calculating deductions and net pay; printing the employee's name, gross pay, deductions, and net pay; and retrieving the name of the next employee to process.

In the flowchart, when a user enters "XXX" for the employee's name, the program exits the While loop and then calls the endOfJob() module. The endOfJob() module is responsible for printing the value of the END_LINE constant. When the endOfJob() module finishes, control returns to the mainline module, and the program stops. The completed Visual Basic program is shown next with the additional statement shown in bold.

You learned about the Convert. ToDouble() method in Chapter 2.

```
Option Explicit On
Option Strict On
Module PayrollReport
    Sub Main()
        Dim name As String
        Dim grossString As String
        Dim gross, deduct, net As Double
        Const RATE As Double = 0.25
        Const QUIT As String = "XXX"
        Const REPORT_HEADING As String = "Payroll Report"
        Const END_LINE As String = "**End of report"

        ' Work done in the housekeeping() procedure
        System.Console.WriteLine(REPORT_HEADING)
        name = InputBox$("Enter employee's name: ")
        While(name <> QUIT)
            ' Work done in the detailLoop() procedure
            grossString = InputBox$( _
                        "Enter employee's gross pay: ")
            gross = Convert.ToDouble(grossString)
            deduct = gross * RATE
            net = gross - deduct
            System.Console.WriteLine("Name: " & name)
            System.Console.WriteLine ("Gross Pay: " & gross)
            System.Console.WriteLine ("Deductions: " & deduct)
            System.Console.WriteLine ("Net Pay: " & net)
            name = InputBox$("Enter employee's name: ")
        End While

        ' Work done in the endOfJob() procedure
        System.Console.WriteLine(END_LINE)
    End Sub
End Module
```

This program is now complete. Figure 3-5 shows the program's output in response to the input "William" (for the name), and 1200 (for the gross).

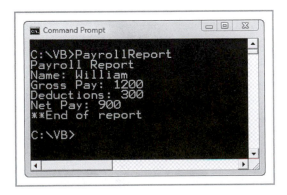

Figure 3-5 Output of the Payroll Report program when the input is "William" and 1200

LAB 3.2 Writing a Modular Program in Visual Basic

In this lab, you add the input and output statements to a partially completed Visual Basic program. When completed, the user should be able to enter a year and then click the "OK" button, enter a month and then click the "OK" button, and enter a day and then click the "OK" button to determine if the date is valid. Valid years are those that are greater than 0, valid months include the values 1 through 12, and valid days include the values 1 through 31.

1. Open the source code file named BadDate.vb using Notepad or the text editor of your choice.

2. Notice that variables have been declared for you.

3. Write the simulated housekeeping() procedure that contains the input statements to retrieve a year, a month, and a day from the user.

4. Add statements to the simulated housekeeping() procedure that convert the String representation of the year, month, and day to Integers.

5. Include the output statements in the simulated endOfJob() procedure. The format of the output is as follows:

   month/day/year is a valid date.

   or

   month/day/year is an invalid date.

6. Save this source code file in a directory of your choice, and then make that directory your working directory.

7. Compile the source code file BadDate.vb.

8. Execute the program entering the following date: month = 7, day = 24, year = 2011. Record the output of this program.

   _____

9. Execute the program entering the following date: month = 9, day = 21, year = 2002. Record the output of this program.

   _____

Writing Programs that Make Decisions

After studying this chapter, you will be able to:

◎ Use comparison and logical Boolean operators to make decisions in a program

◎ Compare numeric and `String` variables

◎ Write decision statements in Visual Basic, including an `If` statement, an `If Then Else` statement, nested `If` statements, and the `Select Case` statement

◎ Use decision statements to make multiple comparisons by using AND logic and OR logic

You should complete the exercises and labs in this chapter only after you have finished Chapter 4 of your book, *Programming Logic and Design, Sixth Edition.* In this chapter, you practice using Visual Basic's comparison and logical operators to write expressions. You also learn the Visual Basic syntax for decision statements, including the If statement, the If Then Else statement, nested If statements, and Select Case statements. Finally, you learn to write Visual Basic statements that make multiple comparisons.

Boolean Operators

You use Boolean operators in expressions when you want to compare values. When you use a **Boolean operator** in an expression, the expression evaluates to either True or False. In Visual Basic, you can subdivide the Boolean operators into two groups: comparison operators and logical operators. We begin the discussion with the comparison operators.

Comparison Operators

When you write Visual Basic programs, you will often want to compare the values stored in variables. For example, you may want to know if one value is greater than another, less than another, or equal to another value. The terms "greater than," "less than," and "equal to" each refer to relationships between two values. As with all Boolean operators, a **comparison operator** allows you to ask a question that results in a True or False answer. The logical path your program takes will depend on the answer to that question. Table 4-1 lists the comparison operators used in Visual Basic.

Operator	Meaning
<	Less than
<=	Less than or equal to
>	Greater than
>=	Greater than or equal to
=	Equal to
<>	Not equal to

Table 4-1   Comparison operators

To see how to use comparison operators, suppose you declare two variables: an Integer named number1 that you initialize with the value 10 and another Integer variable named number2 that you initialize with the value 15. The following code shows the declaration statements for these variables:

```
Dim number1 As Integer = 10
Dim number2 As Integer = 15
```

The following code samples illustrate how comparison operators are used in expressions:

- `number1 < number2` evaluates to `True` because 10 is less than 15.

- `number1 <= number2` evaluates to `True` because 10 is less than or equal to 15.

- `number1 > number2` evaluates to `False` because 10 is not greater than 15.

- `number1 >= number2` evaluates to `False` because 10 is not greater than or equal to 15.

- `number1 = number2` evaluates to `False` because 10 is not equal to 15.

- `number1 <> number2` evaluates to `True` because 10 is not equal to 15.

Logical Operators

You can use another type of Boolean operator, **logical operators**, when you need to ask more than one question but you want to receive only one answer. For example, in a program, you may want to ask if a number is between the values 1 and 10. This actually involves two questions. You need to ask if the number is greater than 1 AND if the number is less than 10. Here, you are asking two questions, but you want only one answer—either "yes" (`True`) or "no" (`False`).

Logical operators are useful in decision statements because, like comparison expressions, they evaluate to `True` or `False`, thereby permitting decision-making in your programs.

Table 4-2 lists the logical operators used in Visual Basic.

Operator	Name	Description
And	AND	All expressions must evaluate to `True` for the entire expression to be `True`.
Or	OR	Only one expression must evaluate to `True` for the entire expression to be `True`.
Not	NOT	This operator reverses the value of the expression; if the expression evaluates to `False`, then reverse it so that the expression evaluates to `True`.

Table 4-2 Logical operators

To see how to use the logical operators, suppose you declare two variables: an `Integer` named `number1` that you initialize with the value 10; and another `Integer` variable named `number2` that you initialize with the value 15. The declaration statements for these variables are shown in the following code:

```
Dim number1 As Integer = 10
Dim number2 As Integer = 15
```

The following code samples illustrate how you can use the logical operators along with the comparison operators in expressions:

- `number1 > number2 Or number1 = 10` evaluates to `True` because the first expression evaluates to `False`, 10 is not greater than 15, and the second expression evaluates to `True`, 10 is equal to 10. Only one expression needs to be `True` using OR logic for the entire expression to be `True`.

- `number1 > number2 And number1 = 10` evaluates to `False` because the first expression is `False`, 10 is not greater than 15, and the second expression is `True`, 10 is equal to 10. Using AND logic, both expressions must be `True` for the entire expression to be `True`. This expression would actually result in a **short-circuit** evaluation. This means that when the first expression, `number1 > number2`, evaluates to `False`, the second expression, `number = 10`, does not need to be evaluated because AND logic dictates that both expressions must be `True` for the entire expression to be `True`.

- `number1 <> number2 And number1 = 10` evaluates to `True` because both expressions are `True`; that is, 10 is not equal to 15, and 10 is equal to 10. Using AND logic, if both expressions are `True`, then the entire expression is `True`.

- `Not number1 = number2` evaluates to `True` because the expression `number1 = number2` evaluates to `False`, 10 is not equal to 15. The `Not` operator then reverses `False`, which results in a `True` value.

Comparison and Logical Operator Precedence and Associativity

Like the arithmetic operators discussed in Chapter 2, the comparison and logical operators are evaluated according to specific rules of associativity and precedence. Table 4-3 shows the precedence and associativity of the operators discussed thus far in this book.

Operator Name	Symbol	Order of Precedence	Associativity
Parentheses	( )	First	Left to right
Exponentiation	^	Second	Left to right
Unary	– +	Third	Right to left
Multiplication, floating point division	* /	Fourth	Left to right
Integer division	\	Fifth	Left to right
Modulus	Mod	Sixth	Left to right
Addition and subtraction	+ –	Seventh	Left to right
Comparison	< > <= >= = <>	Eighth	Left to right
Negation	Not	Ninth	Left to right
AND	And	Tenth	Left to right
OR	Or	Eleventh	Left to right
Assignment	= += –= *= /= \= ^=	Twelfth	Right to left

Table 4-3   Order of precedence and associativity

As shown in Table 4-3, the And operator has a higher precedence than the Or operator, meaning expressions that include the And operator are evaluated first. Also notice that the comparison operators have higher precedence than the And and Or operators. All of these operators have left-to-right associativity.

To see how to use the logical operators and the comparison operators in expressions, first assume that the variables number1 and number2 are declared and initialized as shown in the following code:

```
Dim number1 As Integer = 10
Dim number2 As Integer = 15
```

Next, you write the following expression in Visual Basic:

```
number1 = 8 And number2 = number1 Or number2 = 15
```

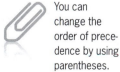

You can change the order of precedence by using parentheses.

Looking at Table 4-3, you can see that the comparison operator (=) has a higher level of precedence than the AND operator (And), and the AND operator (And) has a higher level of precedence than the OR operator (Or). Also, notice that there are three (=) operators in the expression; thus, the left-to-right associativity rule applies. Figure 4-1 illustrates the order in which the operators are used.

As you can see in Figure 4-1, it takes five steps, following the rules of precedence and associativity, to determine the value of the expression.

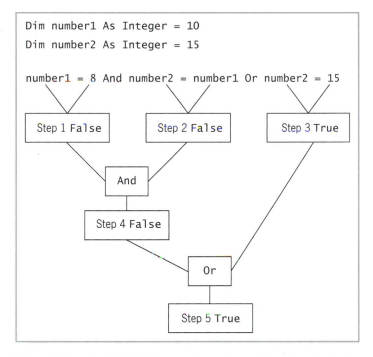

Figure 4-1 Evaluation of expression using relational and logical operators

As you can see in Figure 4-2, when parentheses are added, it still takes five steps, but the order of evaluation is changed, and the result is also changed.

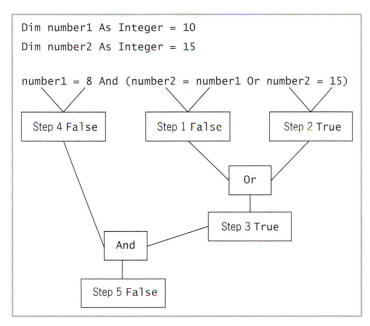

Figure 4-2 Evaluation of expression using relational and logical operators with parentheses added

Comparing Strings

In Visual Basic, you use the same comparison operators when you compare `String` variables that you use to compare numeric data types such as `Integers` and `Doubles`.

The following code shows how to use the equality operator to compare two `String` variables and also to compare one `String` variable and one string constant:

```
Dim s1 As String = "Hello"
Dim s2 As String = "World"
' The following test evaluates to False because "Hello"
' is not the same as "World".
If s1 = s2 Then
    ' code written here executes if True
Else
    ' code written here executes if False
End If
' The following test evaluates to True because "Hello"
' is the same as "Hello".
If s1 = "Hello" Then
    ' code written here executes if True
Else
    ' code written here executes if False
End If

' The following test evaluates to False because "Hello"
' is not the same as "hello".
If s1 = "hello" Then
    ' code written here executes if True
Else
    ' code written here executes if False
End If
```

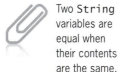 Two `String` variables are equal when their contents are the same.

Visual Basic does not consider a lowercase 'h' to be equal to an uppercase 'H' because their ASCII values are different. Lowercase 'h' has an ASCII value of 104, and uppercase 'H' has an ASCII value of 72. A table of ASCII values can be found in Appendix A: Understanding Numbering Systems and Computer Codes in *Programming Logic and Design, Sixth Edition*.

The following code shows how to use the other comparison operators to compare two `String` variables and also to compare one `String` variable and one string constant:

```
Dim s1 As String = "Hello"
Dim s2 As String = "World"
' The following test evaluates to False because "Hello"
' is not greater than "World".
If s1 > s2 Then
    ' code written here executes if True
Else
    ' code written here executes if False
End If
```

```
' The following test evaluates to True because "Hello"
' is the same as "Hello".
If s1 <= "Hello" Then
    ' code written here executes if True
Else
    ' code written here executes if False
End If
```

When you compare Strings, Visual Basic compares the ASCII values of the individual characters in the String to determine if one String is greater than, less than, or equal to another, in terms of alphabetizing the text in the Strings. As shown in the preceding code, the String variable s1, whose value is "Hello", is not greater than the String variable s2, whose value is "World", because "World" comes after "Hello" in alphabetical order.

The following code sample shows additional examples of using the comparison operators and the equality operator with two String variables:

```
Dim s1 As String = "whole"
Dim s2 As String = "whale"
' The next statement evaluates to True because the
' contents of s1, "whole", are greater than the
' contents of s2, "whale".
If s1 > s2 Then
    ' code written here executes if True
Else
    ' code written here executes if False
End If

' The next statement evaluates to True because the
' contents of s2, "whale", are less than the
' contents of s1, "whole".
If s2 < s1 Then
    ' code written here executes if True
Else
    ' code written here executes if False
End If
' The next statement evaluates to True because the
' contents of s1, "whole", are the same as the
' string constant, "whole".
If s1 = "whole" Then
    ' code written here executes if True
Else
    ' code written here executes if False
End If
```

Decision Statements

Every decision in a program is based on whether an expression evaluates to True or False. Programmers use decision statements to change the flow of control in a program. **Flow of control** means the order in which statements are executed. Decision statements are also known as branching statements because they cause the computer to make a decision, choosing from one or more branches (or paths) in the program.

There are different types of decision statements in Visual Basic. We begin with the `If` statement.

The `If` Statement

The `If` statement is a single-path decision statement. As you learned in *Programming Logic and Design, Sixth Edition*, `If` statements are also referred to as "single alternative" or "single-sided" statements.

When we use the term **single-path**, we mean that if an expression evaluates to `True`, your program executes one or more statements, but if the expression evaluates to `False`, your program will not execute those statements. There is only one defined path—the path taken if the expression evaluates to `True`. In either case, the statement following the `If` statement is executed.

The **syntax**, or set of rules, for writing an `If` statement in Visual Basic is as follows:

```
If expression Then
    statementA
End If
```

Note that when you type the keyword `If` to begin an `If` statement, you follow it with an expression followed by the keyword `Then`.

When the compiler encounters an `If` statement, the expression is evaluated. If the expression evaluates to `True`, then the computer executes *statementA*. If the expression evaluates to `False`, then the computer will not execute *statementA*. Remember that whether the expression evaluates to `True` and executes *statementA*, or the expression evaluates to `False` and does not execute *statementA*, the statement following the `End If` executes next.

Note that a Visual Basic statement, such as an `If` statement, can be either a simple statement or a block statement. A **block statement** is made up of multiple Visual Basic statements. Visual Basic defines a block as multiple statements placed between the `If` and the `End If`. The following example illustrates an `If` statement that uses the comparison operator (<) to test if the value of the variable `customerAge` is less than 65. You will see `If` in the fourth line and the `End If` in the second-to-last line:

```
Dim customerAge As Integer = 53
Dim discount As Integer
Dim numUnder_65 As Integer
If customerAge < 65 Then
    discount = 0
    numUnder_65 += 1
```

```
End If
System.Console.WriteLine("Discount : " & discount)
```

In the preceding code, the variable named `customerAge` is initialized to the value 53. Because 53 is less than 65, the expression `customerAge < 65` evaluates to `True`, and the block statement executes. The block statement is made up of the two assignment statements within the `If` and `End If` statements: `discount = 0` and `numUnder_65 += 1`. If the expression evaluates to `False`, the block statement does not execute. In either case, the next statement to execute is the output statement, `System.Console.WriteLine("Discount : " & discount)`.

The following code uses an `If` statement to test a `String` variable and a string constant for equality:

```
Dim dentPlan As String = "Y"
Dim grossPay As Double
If dentPlan = "Y" Then
    grossPay = grossPay - 23.50
End If
```

In this example, if the value of the `String` variable named `dentPlan` and the string constant "Y" are the same value, the expression evaluates to `True`, and the `grossPay` calculation assignment statement executes. If the expression evaluates to `False`, the `grossPay` calculation assignment statement does not execute.

Exercise 4-1: Understanding If Statements

In this exercise, you use what you have learned about writing `If` statements. Study the following code and then answer Questions 1–4.

```
' VotingAge.vb - This program determines if a person
' is eligible to vote.
Option Explicit On
Option Strict On
Module VotingAge
    Sub Main()
        ' Work done in the housekeeping() procedure
        Dim myAge As Integer = 19
        Dim ableToVote As String = "Yes"
        Const VOTING_AGE As Integer = 18
        ' Work done in the detailLoop() procedure
        If myAge < VOTING_AGE Then
            ableToVote = "No"
        End If
        ' Work done in the endOfJob() procedure
        System.Console.WriteLine("My Age: " & myAge)
        System.Console.WriteLine("Able To Vote: " & _
                            ableToVote)
    End Sub
End Module
```

1. What is the exact output when this program executes?

    _____

    _____

2. What is the exact output if the value of myAge is changed to 15?

    _____

    _____

3. What is the exact output if the expression in the If statement is changed to myAge <= VOTING_AGE?

    _____

    _____

4. What is the exact output if the variable named ableToVote is initialized with the value "No" rather than the value "Yes"?

    _____

    _____

LAB 4.1   Using If Statements

In this lab, you complete a prewritten Visual Basic program for a furniture company. The program is supposed to compute the price of any table a customer orders, based on the following facts:

- The starting price for all tables is $120.00.

- If the surface (length * width) is over 700 square inches, add $40.00.

- If the wood is mahogany, add $250.00; for oak, add $150.00. No charge is added for pine.

- For extension leaves for the table, there is an additional $60.00 charge each.

    1. Open the file named Furniture.vb using Notepad or the text editor of your choice.

    2. You need to declare variables for the following, and initialize them where specified:

        - A variable for the cost of the table initialized to 120.00

        - A variable for the length of the table initialized to 50 inches

        - A variable for the width of the table initialized to 40 inches

- A variable for the surface area of the table

- A variable for the wood type initialized with the value "oak"

- A variable for the number of extension leaves initialized with the value 2

3. Write the rest of the program using assignment statements and If statements as appropriate. The output statements are written for you.

4. Compile the program.

5. Execute the program. Your output should be: The charge for this table is $430.

Note that you do not see a decimal point or digits after the decimal point. You learn how to include a decimal point and specify the number of places after the decimal point in Chapter 9 of this book.

The If Then Else Statement

The If Then Else statement is a dual-path or dual-alternative decision statement. That is, your program will take one of two paths as a result of evaluating an expression in an If Then Else statement.

The syntax for writing an If Then Else statement in Visual Basic is as follows:

```
If expression Then
   statementA
Else
   statementB
End If
```

When the compiler encounters an If Then Else statement, the expression following the keyword If is evaluated. If the expression evaluates to True, then the computer executes *statementA*. Otherwise, if the expression evaluates to False, the computer executes *statementB*. Both *statementA* and *statementB* can be simple statements or block statements. Regardless of which path is taken in a program, the statement following the If Then Else statement is the next one to execute.

The following code sample illustrates an If Then Else statement written in Visual Basic:

```
Dim hoursWorked As Integer = 45
Dim rate As Double = 15.00
```

```
Dim grossPay As Double
Dim overtime As String = "Yes"
Const HOURS_IN_WEEK As Integer = 40
Const OVERTIME_RATE As Double = 1.5
If hoursWorked > HOURS_IN_WEEK Then
    overtime = "Yes"
    grossPay = HOURS_IN_WEEK * rate + _
               (hoursWorked - HOURS_IN_WEEK) _
               OVERTIME_RATE * rate
Else
    overtime = "No"
    grossPay = hoursWorked * rate
End If
System.Console.WriteLine("Overtime: " & overtime)
System.Console.WriteLine("Gross Pay: $ " & grossPay)
```

In the preceding code, the value of the variable named `hoursWorked` is tested to see if it is greater than `HOURS_IN_WEEK`.

HOURS_IN _WEEK is a constant that is initialized with the value 40, and OVERTIME_RATE is a constant that is initialized with the value 1.5.

You use the greater than comparison operator (>) to make the comparison. If the expression `hoursWorked > HOURS_IN_WEEK` evaluates to `True`, then the statement that assigns the string constant "Yes" to the variable named `overtime` executes, followed by another statement that calculates the employee's gross pay, including overtime pay, and assigns the calculated value to the variable named `grossPay`.

If the expression `hoursWorked > HOURS_IN_WEEK` evaluates to `False`, then a different path is followed, and the second block statement following the keyword `Else` executes. This block statement contains one statement that assigns the string constant "No" to the variable named `overtime`, and another statement that calculates the employee's gross pay with no overtime, and assigns the calculated value to the variable named `grossPay`.

Regardless of which path is taken in this code, the next statement to execute is the output statement `System.Console.WriteLine("Overtime: " & overtime)` immediately followed by the output statement `System.Console.WriteLine("Gross Pay: $" & grossPay)`.

Exercise 4-2: Understanding If Then Else Statements

In this exercise, you use what you have learned about writing `If Then Else` statements. This example program was written to calculate customer charges for a telephone company. The telephone company charges 20 cents per minute for calls outside of the customer's area code that last over 15 minutes. All other calls are 25 cents per minute. Study the following code and then answer Questions 1–4.

```vb
' Telephone.vb - This program determines telephone
' call charges.
Option Explicit On
Option Strict On
Module Telephone
    Sub Main()
        ' Work done in the housekeeping() procedure
        Dim custAC As Integer
        Dim custNumber As Integer
        Dim calledAC As Integer
        Dim calledNumber As Integer
        Dim callMinutes As Integer
        Dim callCharge As Double
        Dim MAX_MINS As Integer = 15
        Const CHARGE_1 As Double = 0.20
        Const CHARGE_2 As Double = 0.25
        ' Work done in the detailLoop() procedure

        custAC = 630
        custNumber = 5551234
        calledAC = 219
        calledNumber = 5557890
        callMinutes = 45
        If calledAC <> custAC And callMinutes > MAX_MINS Then
            callCharge = callMinutes * CHARGE_1
        Else
            callCharge = callMinutes * CHARGE_2
        End If
        ' Work done in the endOfJob() procedure

        System.Console.WriteLine("Customer Number: " & _
                    custAC & "-" & custNumber)
        System.Console.WriteLine("Called Number: " & _
                    calledAC & "-" & calledNumber)
        System.Console.WriteLine( _
            "The charge for this call is $" & callCharge)
    End Sub
End Module
```

1. What is the exact output when this program executes?

    _____

    _____

2. What is the exact output if the value of callMinutes is
    changed to 20?

    _____

    _____

3. What is the exact output if the expression in the If statement is changed to callMinutes >= MAX_MINS?

_____

_____

4. What is the exact output if the variable named custAC is assigned the value 219 rather than the value 630?

_____

_____

LAB 4.2 Using If Then Else Statements

In this lab, you complete a prewritten Visual Basic program that computes the largest and smallest of three integer values. The three values are 125, 300, and −10.

1. Open the file named LargeSmall.vb using Notepad or the text editor of your choice.

2. Two variables named largest and smallest are declared for you. Use these variables to store the largest and smallest of the three integer values. You must decide what other variables you will need and initialize them if appropriate.

3. Write the rest of the program using assignment statements, If statements, or If Then Else statements as appropriate. There are comments in the code that tell you where you should write your statements. The output statement is written for you.

4. Compile the program.

5. Execute the program. Your output should be:

The largest value is 300
The smallest value is −10

Nested If Statements

You can nest If statements to create a multipath decision statement. When you nest If statements, you include an If statement within another If statement. This is helpful in programs in which you want to provide more than two possible paths.

The syntax for writing a nested If statement in Visual Basic is as follows:

```
If expressionA Then
    statementA
Else If expressionB Then
    statementB
Else
    statementC
End If
```

This is called a nested If statement because the second If statement is a part of the first If statement. This is easier to see if the example is changed as follows:

```
If expressionA Then
    statementA
Else
    If expressionB Then
        statementB
    Else
        statementC
    End If
End If
```

Now let's see how a nested If statement works. As shown in Figure 4-3, if *expressionA* evaluates to True, then the computer executes *statementA*. If *expressionA* evaluates to False, then the computer will evaluate *expressionB*. If *expressionB* evaluates to True, then the computer will execute *statementB*. If both *expressionA* and *expressionB* evaluate to False, then the computer will execute *statementC*. Regardless of which path is taken in this code, the statement following the If Then Else statement is the next one to execute.

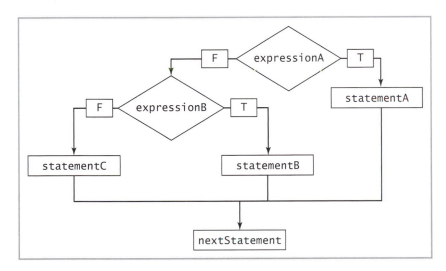

Figure 4-3 Evaluation of a nested If statement

The Visual Basic code sample that follows illustrates a nested `If` statement:

```
If empDept <= 3 Then
    supervisorName = "Dillon"
Else If empDept <= 7 Then
    supervisorName = "Escher"
Else
    supervisorName = "Fontana"
End If
System.Console.WriteLine("Supervisor: " & supervisorName)
```

When you read the preceding code, you can assume that a department number is never less than 1. If the value of the variable named `empDept` is less than or equal to the value 3 (in the range of values from 1 to 3), then the value "Dillon" is assigned to the variable named `supervisorName`. If the value of `empDept` is not less than or equal to 3, but it is less than or equal to 7 (in the range of values from 4 to 7), then the value "Escher" is assigned to the variable named `supervisorName`. If the value of `empDept` is not in the range of values from 1 to 7, then the value "Fontana" is assigned to the variable named `supervisorName`. As you can see, there are three possible paths this program could take when the nested `If` statement is encountered. Regardless of which path the program takes, the next statement to execute is the output statement `System.Console.WriteLine("Supervisor: " & supervisorName)`.

Exercise 4-3: Understanding Nested `If` Statements

In this exercise, you use what you have learned about writing nested `If` statements. This example program was written for the Woof Wash dog-grooming business to calculate a total charge for services rendered. Woof Wash charges $20 for a bath, $10 for a cut, and $8 to trim nails. Study the following code and then answer Questions 1–3.

```
' WoofWash.vb - This program determines if a doggy
' service is provided and prints the charge.
Option Explicit On
Option Strict On
Module WoofWash
    Sub Main()
        ' Work done in the housekeeping() procedure
        Dim service As String
        Const SERVICE_1 As String = "bath"
        Const SERVICE_2 As String = "cut"
        Const SERVICE_3 As String = "trim nails"
        Dim charge As Double
        Const BATH_CHARGE As Double = 20.00
        Const CUT_CHARGE As Double = 10.00
```

```
        Const NAIL_CHARGE As Double = 8.00
        service = InputBox$("Enter service: ")
        ' Work done in the detailLoop() procedure
        If service = SERVICE_1 Then
          charge = BATH_CHARGE
        Else If service = SERVICE_2 Then
          charge = CUT_CHARGE
        Else If service = SERVICE_3 Then
          charge = NAIL_CHARGE
        Else
          charge = 0.00
        End If
        ' Work done in the endOfJob() procedure
        If charge > 0.00 Then
          System.Console.WriteLine( _
                    "The charge for a doggy " & _
                    service & " is $" & charge & ".")
        Else
          System.Console.WriteLine( _
                    "We do not perform the " & _
                    service & " service.")
        End If
      End Sub
End Module
```

1. What is the exact output when this program executes if the user enters "bath"?

    _____

    _____

2. What is the exact output when this program executes if the user enters "shave"?

    _____

    _____

3. What is the exact output when this program executes if the user enters "BATH"?

    _____

    _____

LAB 4.3 Using Nested If Statements

In this lab, you complete a prewritten Visual Basic program that calculates an employee's end-of-year bonus and prints the employee's name, yearly salary, performance rating, and bonus. Bonuses are calculated based on an employee's annual salary and his or her performance rating. The rating system is contained in Table 4-4.

Rating	Bonus
1	15% of annual salary
2	10% of annual salary
3	6% of annual salary
4	None

Table 4-4   Employee ratings and bonuses

1. Open the file named `EmployeeBonus.vb` using Notepad or the text editor of your choice.

2. Variables have been declared for you, and the input statements and output statements have been written. Read them over carefully before you proceed to the next step.

3. Design the logic and write the rest of the program using a nested `If Then Else` statement.

4. Compile the program.

5. Execute the program entering the following as input:

   Employee's name: Laurie Blair
   Employee's salary: 65000.00
   Employee's performance rating: 3

6. Your output should be:

   Employee Name: Laurie Blair
   Employee Salary: $65000
   Employee Rating: 3
   Employee Bonus: $3900

You learn how to insert a decimal point and to control the number of places that appear after the decimal point in Chapter 9 of this book.

The `Select Case` Statement

The `Select Case` statement is similar to a nested `If` statement because it is also a multipath decision statement. A `Select Case` statement offers the advantage of being easier for you to read than nested `If` statements, and a `Select Case` statement is also easier for you, the programmer, to maintain. You use the `Select Case` statement in situations when you want to compare an expression with several numeric or string constants.

The syntax for writing a `Select Case` statement in Visual Basic is as follows:

```
Select Case testexpression
    Case expressionlist1
      statement(s)
    Case expressionlist2
      statement(s)
    Case expressionlist3
      statement(s)
    Case Else
      statement(s)
End Select
```

You begin writing a `Select Case` statement with the keywords `Select Case`. Following `Select Case`, you include an expression that evaluates to a numeric or string value. Cases are then defined within the `Select Case` statement by using the keyword `Case` as a label, and including a numeric or string value after this label. For example, you could include an integer constant such as 10 or an arithmetic expression that evaluates to an integer such as 10/2. You could also include a string constant such as "Hello". The computer evaluates the *testexpression* in the `Select Case` statement and then compares it to the *expressionlist* values following the `Case` labels. If the *testexpression* and an *expressionlist* value match, then the computer executes the statement(s) that follow until it encounters the next `Case` label or the `End Select` statement. You can use the keyword `Else` to establish a case for values that do not match any of the *expressionlist* values following the `Case` labels.

If the *test expression* matches more than one *expressionlist* value, only the statement(s) following the first match are executed.

The following code sample illustrates the use of the `Select Case` statement in Visual Basic:

```
Dim deptNum As Integer
Dim deptName As String
deptName = "Development"
Select Case deptName
    Case "Marketing"
      deptNum = 1
    Case "Development"
        deptNum = 2
    Case "Sales"
        deptNum = 3
    Case Else
        deptNum = 0
End Select
System.Console.WriteLine("Department: " & deptNum)
```

In the preceding example, when the program encounters the `Select Case` statement, the value of the variable named `deptName` is "Development". The value "Development" matches the string constant in the second case of the Select Case statement. Therefore, the value 2 is assigned to the Integer variable named deptNum. A Case label is encountered next, and causes the program to exit from the Select Case statement. The statement following the Select Case statement System.Console.WriteLine("Department: " & deptNum) executes next.

In Visual Basic, the *expressionlist* can be made up of one or more of the following:

- expression(s)

- expression To expression

- Is comparison operator expression

The following code sample illustrates the use of various forms of the *expressionlist* in the Select Case statement in Visual Basic:

```
Dim yearsOfService As Integer
Dim vacationDays As Integer
yearsOfService = 22
Select Case yearsOfService
    Case 1 To 10
        vacationDays = 10
    Case 11 To 14
        vacationDays = 15
    Case 15 To 19
        vacationDays = 20
    Case Is >= 20
        vacationDays = 25
    Case Else
        vacationDays = 0
End Select
System.Console.WriteLine("Vacation Days: " & vacationDays)
```

You can also include multiple values in an *expressionlist* by including a comma between the values as follows: Case 1, 3, 5.

In the preceding example, when the program encounters the Select Case statement, the value of the variable named yearsOfService is 22. The program then encounters the first case, which is Case 1 To 10. The value of yearsOfService is not in the range of 1 through 10 so the program then tests the second case, which is Case 11 To 14. The value of yearsOfService is not in the range of 11 through 14 so the program then tests the third case, which is Case 15 To 19. The value of yearsOfService is not in the range of 15 through 19 so the program then tests the fourth case, which is Case Is >= 20. The value of yearsOfService is greater than or equal to 20. Therefore, the value 25 is assigned to the Integer variable named vacationDays. A Case label is encountered next, and causes the program to exit from the Select Case statement. The statement following the Select Case statement System.Console.WriteLine("Vacation Days: " & vacationDays) executes next.

Exercise 4-4: Using a Select Case Statement

In this exercise, you use what you have learned about the Select Case statement. Study the following code and then answer Questions 1–4.

First, examine the following code:

```
Dim numValue As Integer = 20
Dim answer As Integer = 0
Select Case numValue
    Case 10
      answer = answer + 10
    Case 20
      answer = answer + 20
    Case 30
      answer = answer + 30
    Case 40
      answer = answer + 40
    Case 50
      answer = answer + 50
    Case Else
      answer = 0
End Select
System.Console.WriteLine("Answer: " & answer)
```

1. What is the value of answer if the value of numValue is 20?

    _____

2. What is the value of answer if the value of numValue is 40?

    _____

3. What is the value of answer if the value of numValue is 10?

    _____

4. What is the value of answer if the value of numValue is 22?

    _____

LAB 4.4   Using a Select Case Statement

In this lab, you complete a prewritten Visual Basic program that calculates an employee's end-of-year bonus and prints the employee's name, yearly salary, performance rating, and bonus. This is the same program you wrote in Lab 4.3 when you used nested If statements to write the program. This time you use a Select Case statement instead of nested If statements.

In this program, bonuses are calculated based on employees' annual salary and their performance rating. The rating system is contained in Table 4-5.

Rating	Bonus
1	15% of annual salary
2	10% of annual salary
3	6% of annual salary
4	None

Table 4-5   Employee ratings and bonuses

1. Open the file named EmployeeBonus2.vb using Notepad or the text editor of your choice.

2. Variables have been declared for you, and the input statements and output statements have been written. Read them over carefully before you proceed to the next step.

3. Design the logic and write the rest of the program using a Select Case statement.

4. Compile the program.

5. Execute the program entering the following as input:

   Employee's name: Laurie Blair
   Employee's salary: 65000.00
   Employee's performance rating: 3

6. Confirm that your output matches the following:

   Employee Name: Laurie Blair
   Employee Salary: $65000
   Employee Rating: 3
   Employee Bonus: $3900

Using Decision Statements to Make Multiple Comparisons

When you write programs, you must often write statements that include multiple comparisons. For example, you may want to determine that two conditions are True before you decide which path your program will take. In the following sections, you learn how to implement AND logic in a program by using the AND (And) logical operator. You also learn how to implement OR logic using the OR (Or) logical operator.

Using AND Logic

When you write Visual Basic programs, you can use the AND operator (And) to make multiple comparisons in a single decision statement. Remember that when using AND logic, all expressions must evaluate to True for the entire expression to be True.

The Visual Basic code that follows illustrates a decision statement that uses the AND operator (And) to implement AND logic:

```
Dim medicalPlan As String = "Y"
Dim dentalPlan As String = "Y"
If medicalPlan = "Y" And dentalPlan = "Y" Then
    System.Console.WriteLine( _
            "Employee has medical insurance" & _
            " and also has dental insurance.")
Else
    System.Console.WriteLine( _
            "Employee may have medical insurance " & _
            "or may have dental insurance, but does " & _
            "not have both medical and dental " & _
            "insurance.")
End If
```

In this example, the variables named medicalPlan and dentalPlan have both been initialized to the string constant "Y". When the expression medicalPlan = "Y" is evaluated, the result is True. When the expression dentalPlan = "Y" is evaluated, the result is also True. Because both expressions evaluate to True, the entire expression medicalPlan = "Y" And dentalPlan = "Y" evaluates to True. Because the entire expression is True, the output generated is "Employee has medical insurance and also has dental insurance."

If you initialize either of the variables medicalPlan or dentalPlan with a value other than "Y", then the expression medicalPlan = "Y" And dentalPlan = "Y" evaluates to False, and the output generated is "Employee may have medical insurance or may have dental insurance, but does not have both medical and dental insurance."

Using OR Logic

You can use OR logic when you want to make multiple comparisons in a single decision statement. Of course, you must remember when using OR logic that only one expression must evaluate to True for the entire expression to be True.

The Visual Basic code that follows illustrates a decision statement that uses the OR operator (Or) to implement OR logic:

```
Dim medicalPlan As String = "Y"
Dim dentalPlan As String = "N"
If medicalPlan = "Y" Or dentalPlan = "Y"
    System.Console.WriteLine( _
        "Employee has medical insurance" & _
        " or dental insurance or both.")
Else
    System.Console.WriteLine( _
        "Employee does not have medical" & _
        " insurance and also does not have dental insurance.")
End If
```

In this example, the variable named medicalPlan is initialized to the string constant "Y", and the variable named dentalPlan is initialized to the string constant "N". When the expression medicalPlan = "Y" is evaluated, the result is True. When the expression dentalPlan = "Y" is evaluated, the result is False. The expression medicalPlan = "Y" Or dentalPlan = "Y" evaluates to True because when using OR logic, only one of the expressions must evaluate to True for the entire expression to be True. Because the entire expression is True, the output generated is "Employee has medical insurance or dental insurance or both."

If you initialize both of the variables medicalPlan and dentalPlan to the string constant "N", then the expression medicalPlan = "Y" Or dentalPlan = "Y" evaluates to False, and the output generated is "Employee does not have medical insurance and also does not have dental insurance."

Exercise 4-5: Making Multiple Comparisons in Decision Statements

In this exercise, you use what you have learned about OR logic. This example program was written for a marketing research firm that wants to determine if a customer prefers Coke or Pepsi over some other drink. Study the following code and then answer Questions 1–4.

```
' CokeOrPepsi.vb - This program determines if a customer
' prefers to drink Coke or Pepsi or some other drink.
Option Explicit On
Option Strict On
Module CokeOrPepsi
    Sub Main()
        Dim customerName As String ' Customer's name
        Dim drink As String = "" ' Customer's favorite drink
```

```
' Work done in the housekeeping() procedure
customerName = InputBox$("Enter customer's name: ")
drink = InputBox$( _
        "Enter customer's drink preference: ")
' Work done in the detailLoop() procedure
If drink = "Coke" Or drink = "Pepsi" Then
   System.Console.WriteLine("Customer Name: " & _
                            customerName)
   System.Console.WriteLine("Drink: " & drink)
Else
   System.Console.WriteLine(customerName & _
                " does not prefer Coke or Pepsi.")
End If
    End Sub
End Module
```

1. What is the exact output when this program executes if the customer's name is "Sally Preston" and the drink is "Pepsi"?

    _____

    _____

2. What is the exact output when this program executes if the customer's name is "Sally Preston" and the drink is "Coke"?

    _____

    _____

3. What is the exact output from this program when

    ```
    If drink = "Coke" Or drink = "Pepsi"
    ```

    is changed to

    ```
    If drink = "Coke" And drink = "Pepsi"
    ```

    and the customer's name is still "Sally Preston" and the drink is still "Coke"?

    _____

    _____

4. What is the exact output from this program when

    ```
    If drink = "Coke" Or drink = "Pepsi"
    ```

    is changed to

    ```
    If drink = "Coke" Or drink = "Pepsi" Or drink = "coke" _
            Or drink = "pepsi"
    ```

and the customer's name is "Sally Preston", and the drink is "pepsi"? What does this change allow a user to enter?

_____

_____

LAB 4.5 Making Multiple Comparisons in Decision Statements

In this lab, you complete a partially written Visual Basic program for an airline that offers a 10% discount to passengers who are 12 years old or younger and the same discount to passengers who are 65 years old or older. The program should request a passenger's name and age, and then print whether the passenger is eligible or not eligible for a discount.

1. Open the file named `Airline.vb` using Notepad or the text editor of your choice.

2. Variables have been declared and initialized for you, and the input statements have been written. Read them carefully before you proceed to the next step.

3. Design the logic, deciding whether to use AND or OR logic. Write the decision statement to identify when a discount should be offered and when a discount should not be offered.

4. Be sure to include output statements telling whether or not the customer is eligible for a discount.

5. Compile the program.

6. Execute the program, entering the following as input:

    a. Customer Name: Connie Chen
        Customer Age: 22
        What is the output?

        _____

    b. Customer Name: William Gorman
        Customer Age: 66
        What is the output?

        _____

c. Customer Name: Maria Gonzales
    Customer Age: 72
    What is the output?

    _____

d. Customer Name: Sheila Morton
    Customer Age: 52
    What is the output?

    _____

e. Customer Name: Timmy Morton
    Customer Age: 2
    What is the output?

    _____

f. Customer Name: Helen Patel
    Customer Age: 12
    What is the output?

    _____

Writing Programs Using Loops

After studying this chapter, you will be able to:

◎ Recognize how and when to use `Do While` loops in Visual Basic, including how to use a counter and how to use a sentinel value to control a loop

◎ Use `For` loops in Visual Basic

◎ Write `Do Until` loops in Visual Basic

◎ Include nested loops in applications

◎ Accumulate totals by using a loop in a Visual Basic application

◎ Use a loop to validate user input in an application

In this chapter, you learn how to use Visual Basic to program three types of loops: a Do While loop, a For loop, and a Do Until loop. You also learn how to nest loops, how to use a loop to help you accumulate a total in your programs, and how to use a loop to validate user input.

You should do the exercises and labs in this chapter only after you have finished Chapter 5 in your book, *Programming Logic and Design, Sixth Edition*. In that chapter, you learned that loops allow a programmer to direct the computer to execute a statement or a group of statements multiple times. In other words, loops allow a programmer to change the flow of control in a program.

Writing a Do While Loop in Visual Basic

As you learned in *Programming Logic and Design, Sixth Edition*, three steps must occur in every loop:

1. You must initialize a variable that will control the loop. This variable is known as the **loop control variable**.

2. You must compare the loop control variable to some value, known as the **sentinel value**, which decides whether the loop continues or stops. This decision is based on a Boolean comparison. The result of a Boolean comparison is always a True or False value.

3. Within the loop, you must alter the value of the loop control variable.

You also learned that the statements that are part of a loop are referred to as the **loop body**. In Visual Basic, the loop body may consist of a single statement or a block statement.

The statements that make up the loop body may be any type of statements, including assignment statements, decision statements, or even other loops. Note that the Visual Basic syntax for writing a Do While loop is as follows:

```
Do While expression
    statement(s)
Loop
```

The Do While loop allows you to direct the computer to execute the statement(s) in the body of the loop as long as the expression evaluates to True.

 The body of a Do While loop will not execute even once if the condition is False the first time it is evaluated.

Study the following Do While loop, which uses a block statement as its loop body. (Note that the line numbers in this example are not part of the Visual Basic code. They are included for reference only.)

```
1 Const NUM_TIMES As Integer = 3
2 num = 0
3 Do While num < NUM_TIMES
4     System.Console.WriteLine( _
5              "Welcome to Visual Basic Programming.")
6     num = num + 1
7 Loop
```

In this example, a block statement is used because the loop body (lines 4, 5, and 6) contains more than one statement. The loop begins on line 3 with the comparison num < NUM_TIMES. The first time through the loop, the value of num is 0. The 0 is compared to and found to be less than the value of NUM_TIMES, which is 3. This means the condition is True, so the first statement of the block (lines 4 and 5) executes, causing the text "Welcome to Visual Basic Programming." to appear on the user's screen.

The second statement of the block (line 6), num = num + 1, is important because it causes num, the loop control variable, to increase by 1. Thus, the second time through the loop, the value of num is 1. Because this is still less than 3, the text appears a second time. Next, the statement num = num + 1 again increases the value of num by 1. Therefore, the third comparison also results in a True value (because the value of num is now 2, which is still less than 3). As a result, the text appears a third time, and 1 is added to num again. Finally, the fourth time the comparison is made, the value of num is 3, which is not less than 3; as a result, the program exits the loop.

Exercise 5-1: Using a Do While Loop

In this exercise, you use what you have learned about writing Do While loops. Study the following code and then answer Questions 1–3.

```
Const NUM_LOOPS As Integer = 7
Dim numberOfTimes As Integer = NUM_LOOPS
Do While numberOfTimes < NUM_LOOPS
   System.Console.WriteLine("Value of numberOfTimes is " _
           & numberOfTimes)
   numberOfTimes = numberOfTimes + 1
Loop
```

1. What is the loop control variable?

   _____

2. What is the output?

   _____

3. What is the output if the code is changed to `Do While numberOfTimes <= NUM_LOOPS`?

Using a Counter to Control a Loop

In Chapter 5 of *Programming Logic and Design, Sixth Edition*, you learned that you can use a counter to control a `Do While` loop. With a counter, you set up the loop to execute a specified number of times. Also recall that a `Do While` loop may execute zero times if the expression used in the comparison immediately evaluates to `False`. In that case, the computer does not execute the body of the loop at all.

Chapter 5 of *Programming Logic and Design, Sixth Edition* discusses a counter-controlled loop that controls how many times the word "Hello" is printed. Let's take a look at the following pseudocode for this counter-controlled loop:

```
start
   Declarations
      num count = 0
   while count < 4
      print "Hello"
      count = count + 1
   endwhile
         output "Goodbye"
   stop
```

The counter for this loop is a variable named `count`, which is assigned the value 0. The Boolean expression `count < 4` is tested to see if the value of `count` is less than 4. If `True`, the loop executes. If `False`, the program exits the loop. If the loop executes, the program displays the word "Hello", and then adds 1 to the value of `count`. The loop body executes four times, and the word "Hello" is displayed four times. When the loop is exited, the word "Goodbye" is displayed.

Now, let's see what the code looks like when you translate the pseudocode to Visual Basic:

```
Dim count As Integer = 0
Do While count < 4
   System.Console.WriteLine("Hello")
   count = count + 1
Loop
System.Console.WriteLine("Goodbye")
```

First, the variable `count` is initialized with a value of 0 and is used as the counter to control the `Do While` loop. The `Do While` loop follows and includes the Boolean expression `count < 4`. The counter-controlled loop executes two statements that display the word "Hello" and then adds 1 to the value of `count`. When the loop is exited, the word "Goodbye" is displayed.

 Adding 1 to the `count` variable is important. Each time through the loop, the value of `count` must be increased by 1 or the expression `count < 4` would never be `False`. This would result in an **infinite** loop, which is a loop that never ends.

Exercise 5-2: Using a Counter-Controlled Do While Loop

In this exercise, you use what you have learned about counter-controlled loops. Study the following code and then answer Questions 1–3.

> Remember that number2 += number1 is the same as number2 = number2 + number1.

```
Dim number1 As Integer = 0
Dim number2 As Integer = 0
Do While number1 < 8
    number1 = number1 + 1
Loop
number2 += number1
```

1. What is the value of number1 when the loop exits?

   _____

2. What is the value of number2 when the loop exits?

   _____

3. Other than assigning the value 36 to the variable named number2, what could you do to force the value of number2 to be 36 when the loop exits?

   _____

LAB 5.1 Using a Counter-Controlled Do While Loop

In this lab, you use a counter-controlled Do While loop in a Visual Basic program provided with the data files for this book. When completed, the program should print the numbers 0 through 10, along with their values doubled and quadrupled (multiplied by four). The file contains the necessary variable declarations and output statements.

1. Open the source code file named DoubleQuadruple.vb using Notepad or the text editor of your choice.

2. Write a counter-controlled Do While loop that uses the loop control variable to take on the values 0 through 10. Remember to initialize the loop control variable before the program enters the loop.

3. In the body of the loop, calculate the double and the quadruple using the value of the loop control variable. Remember to change the value of the loop control variable in the body of the loop.

4. Save the source code file in a directory of your choice, and then make that directory your working directory.

5. Compile the source code file `DoubleQuadruple.vb`.

6. Execute the program. Record the output of this program.

Using a Sentinel Value to Control a Loop

As you learned in Chapter 1 of *Programming Logic and Design, Sixth Edition*, a sentinel value is a value such as "Y" or "N" that a user must supply to stop a loop. To learn about sentinel values in Visual Basic, we will look at a program discussed in Chapter 5 of *Programming Logic and Design, Sixth Edition* and in Chapter 3 of this book. The program creates a payroll report for a small company. This program includes a `Do While` loop and uses a sentinel value to determine when the loop executes or when the loop is exited. The pseudocode is shown below.

```
start
   Declarations
      string name
      num gross
      num deduct
      num net
      num RATE = 0.25
      string QUIT = "XXX"
      string REPORT_HEADING = "Payroll Report"
      string COLUMN_HEADING = "Name   Gross   Deductions   Net"
      string END_LINE = "**End of report"
   housekeeping()
   while not name = QUIT
      detailLoop()
   endwhile
   endOfJob()
stop

housekeeping()
   output REPORT_HEADING
   output COLUMN_HEADING
   input name
return

detailLoop()
   input gross
   deduct = gross * RATE
   net = gross - deduct
   output name, gross, deduct, net
   input name
return

endOfJob()
   output END_LINE
return
```

Figure 5-1 Pseudocode for a payroll report program

80

Note that a **priming read** is included in the housekeeping() method in the pseudocode shown in Figure 5-1. Recall that you perform a priming read before a loop executes to input a value that is then used to control the loop. When a priming read is used, the program must perform another read within the loop body to get the next input value. You can see the priming read, the loop, and the last output statement portion of the pseudocode translated to Visual Basic in the following code sample:

```
name = InputBox$("Enter employee's name or XXX to quit: ")
Do While name <> QUIT
    ' This is the work done in the detailLoop() procedure
    grossString = InputBox$("Enter employee's gross pay: ")
    gross = Convert.ToDouble(grossString)
    deduct = gross * RATE
    net = gross - deduct
    System.Console.WriteLine("Name: " & name)
    System.Console.WriteLine("Gross Pay: " & gross)
    System.Console.WriteLine("Deductions: " & deduct)
    System.Console.WriteLine("Net Pay: " & net)
    name = InputBox$( _
            "Enter employee's name or XXX to quit: ")
Loop
System.Console.WriteLine(END_LINE)
```

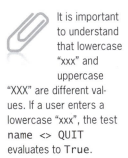 It is important to understand that lowercase "xxx" and uppercase "XXX" are different values. If a user enters a lowercase "xxx", the test name <> QUIT evaluates to True.

In this code example, the variable named name is the loop control variable. It is assigned a value when the program instructs the user to "Enter employee's name or XXX to quit: " and reads the user's response. The loop control variable is tested with name <> QUIT. If the user enters a name (any value other than "XXX", which is the constant value of QUIT), then the test expression is True, and the statements within the loop body execute. If the user enters "XXX" (the constant value of QUIT), which is the sentinel value, then the test expression is False, and the loop is exited.

The first statement instructs the user to enter an employee's gross pay. The program then retrieves the user's input and stores it in the String variable named grossString and then coverts the String to a Double and stores it in the variable named gross. The employee's deductions are calculated next and stored in the variable named deduct followed by the program calculating the employee's net pay and storing the value in the variable named net. Next, the program outputs the name of the employee followed by the employee's gross pay, deductions, and net pay.

The last statement in the loop prompts the user for a new value for name. This is the statement that may change the value of the loop control variable. The loop body ends when program control returns to the top of the loop, where the Boolean expression in the Do While statement is tested again. If the user enters a name at the last prompt, then the loop is entered again. If the user enters "XXX", then the test expression is False, and the loop body doesn't execute. When the loop is exited, the next statement to execute displays "**End of report" (the constant value of END_LINE).

Exercise 5-3: Using a Sentinel Value to Control a Do While Loop

In this exercise, you use what you have learned about sentinel values. Study the following code, and then answer Questions 1–4.

```
stringNumToPrint = InputBox$( _
                    "How many pages do you want to print?")
numToPrint = Convert.ToInt32(stringNumToPrint)
counter = 1
Do While counter <= numToPrint
   System.Console.WriteLine("Page Number " & counter)
Loop
counter = counter + 1
System.Console.WriteLine("Value of counter is " & counter)
```

1. What is the output if the user enters an 8?

    _____

2. What is the problem with this code, and how can you fix it?

    _____

3. Assuming you fix the problem, if the user enters 100 as the number of pages to print, what is the value of counter when the loop exits?

    _____

4. Assuming you fix the problem, if the user enters 0 as the number of pages to print, how many pages will print?

    _____

LAB 5.2 Using a Sentinel Value to Control a Do While Loop

In this lab, you write a Do While loop that uses a sentinel value to control a loop in a Visual Basic program provided with the data files for this book. You also write the statements that make up the body of the loop. The source code file already contains the necessary variable declarations and output statements. When completed, the program should print a payoff schedule for a credit card company customer. At the beginning of every month, 1.2%

interest is added to the balance, and then the customer makes a payment equal to 5% of the current balance. When the balance reaches $10.00 or less, the customer can pay off the account. As you will see, this program generates a lot of output, even for one customer.

1. Open the source code file named `Payoff.vb` using Notepad or the text editor of your choice.

2. Write the `Do While` loop using a sentinel value to control the loop, and also write the statements that make up the body of the loop.

3. Save this source code file in a directory of your choice, and then make that directory your working directory.

4. Compile the source code file `Payoff.vb`.

5. Execute the program. Input the following:

    Account Number: 6789A
    Customer Name: Jeanne Johnson
    Balance: 120.00

6. Record the final balance amount when the loan may be paid off.

Writing a For Loop in Visual Basic

In Chapter 5 of *Programming Logic and Design, Sixth Edition*, you learned that a `For` loop is a **definite** loop. In other words, this type of loop executes a definite number of times. The following is the syntax for a `For` loop in Visual Basic:

```
For counter variable = start value To end value
    statement(s)
Next counter variable
```

In Visual Basic, the `For` loop begins with the keyword `For` followed by the name of an `Integer` variable that is initialized with a start value and is used as a counter. The keyword `To` comes next, followed by an end value. The `For` loop executes as follows:

- The first time the `For` loop is encountered, the start value is assigned to the counter variable that is used to control the `For` loop.

- Next, the value stored in the counter variable is compared to the end value. If the value of the counter variable is less than or equal to the end value, the result of the comparison is `True`, and the loop statement(s) executes. If the result is `False`, the loop is exited.

- The statement that marks the end of the For loop includes the keyword Next followed by the name of the counter variable. When this statement executes, it causes 1 to be added to the current value of the counter variable.

- Next, the current value of the counter variable is again compared to the end value. If the result is still True, the loop statement(s) executes again, and 1 is again added to the counter variable.

- This process continues until the comparison results in a False value, causing an exit from the loop.

The following code sample illustrates a Visual Basic For loop:

```
Dim number As Integer = 0
Dim count As Integer
Const NUM_LOOPS As Integer = 10
For count = 1 To NUM_LOOPS
    number += count
    System.Console.WriteLine("Value of number is: " & number)
Next count
```

Notice that the assignment statement count = 1 is not needed before the For loop is entered as this is accomplished as part of the For loop itself.

In this For loop example, the variable named count is initialized to 1 when the loop is first encountered.

When the value of count is compared to NUM_LOOPS the first time, the value of count is 1. Because this is less than or equal to the value of NUM_LOOPS, which is 10, the result is True. The loop statements are then executed. This is where a new value is computed and assigned to the variable named number and then is displayed. The first time through the loop, the output is as follows: Value of number is: 1.

After the output is displayed, the Next statement executes; this adds 1 to the value of count, making the new value of count equal to 2. When the value of count is compared to NUM_LOOPS a second time, the value of count is 2. The result is a True value and causes the loop statements to execute again where a new value is computed for number and then displayed. The second time through the loop, the output is as follows: Value of number is: 3.

The Next statement then adds 1 to the value of count. The value of count is now 3. The value of count is compared to the value of NUM_LOOPS a third time. Again, the result of the comparison is True because 3 is less than or equal to NUM_LOOPS. The third time through, the loop body changes the value of number, and then displays the new value. The output is as follows: Value of number is: 6.

This process continues until the value of count becomes 11. At this time, 11 is not less than or equal to NUM_LOOPS, so the comparison results in a False value. Thus, the For loop ends.

Let's return to the counter-controlled loop that displays the word "Hello" four times (which you studied in the "Using a Counter to Control a Loop" section of this chapter). We can rewrite this using a For loop instead of the Do While loop. In fact, when you know how many times a loop will execute, it is considered a good programming practice to use a For loop instead of a Do While loop.

To rewrite the Do While loop as a For loop, you first delete the assignment statement counter = 0 because you initialize counter as part of the For loop. The program continues to print the word "Hello" and adding 1 to the value of counter in the body of the loop. The following code sample illustrates this For loop:

```
Dim counter As Integer
Const NUM_LOOPS As Integer = 3
For counter = 0 To NUM_LOOPS
    System.Console.WriteLine("Hello")
Next counter
```

Exercise 5-4: Using a For Loop

In this exercise, you use what you have learned about For loops. Study the following code, and then answer Questions 1–3.

```
Const NUM_LOOPS As Integer = 26
Dim numTimes As Integer
For numTimes = 1 TO NUM_LOOPS
    System.Console.WriteLine("Value of numTimes is: " & _
                                numTimes)
    numTimes = numTimes + 1
Next numTimes
```

Answer the following three questions with "True" or "False":

1. This loop executes 26 times.

   _____

2. This loop could be written as a Do While loop.

   _____

3. This loop executes 13 times.

   _____

LAB 5.3   Using a For Loop

In this lab, you work with the same Visual Basic program you worked with in Lab 5.1. As in Lab 5.1, the completed program should print the numbers 0 through 10, along with their values doubled and quadrupled. However, in this lab you should accomplish this using a For loop instead of a counter-controlled Do While loop.

1. Open the source code file named NewDoubleQuadruple.vb using Notepad or the text editor of your choice.

2. Write a For loop that uses the loop control variable to take on the values 0 through 10.

3. In the body of the loop, calculate the double and the quadruple using the value of the loop control variable.

4. Save this source code file in a directory of your choice, and then make that directory your working directory.

5. Compile the source code file NewDoubleQuadruple.vb.

6. Execute the program. Is the output the same as in Lab 5.1?

Writing a Do Until Loop in Visual Basic

In Chapter 5 of *Programming Logic and Design, Sixth Edition*, you learned about the Do Until loop. The Do Until loop uses logic that can be summarized as follows: do A until B is true. This is similar to as a Do While loop; however, there is a difference. When you use a Do While loop, the statements in the loop body execute as long as the condition that is tested evaluates to True. When you use a Do Until loop, the statements in the loop body execute as long as the condition evaluates to False. The Do Until syntax is as follows:

```
Do Until expression
   statement(s)
Loop
```

The following Do Until loop is a revised version of the Do While loop you saw earlier, which prints the word "Hello" four times. In this version, the loop is rewritten as a Do Until loop.

```
Dim counter As Integer = 0
Const NUM_LOOPS As Integer = 4
Do Until counter = NUM_LOOPS
   System.Console.WriteLine("Hello")
   counter = counter + 1
Loop
```

In this example, notice that you use Visual Basic statements in the body of Do Until loops just as in Do While and For loops. When this loop is encountered, the value of counter is compared with the constant NUM_LOOPS. As long as the value of counter is not equal to NUM_LOOPS, the word "Hello" is printed, and 1 is added to the value of counter.

Exercise 5-5: Using a Do Until Loop

In this exercise, you use what you have learned about Do Until loops. Study the following code and then answer Questions 1–4.

```
Const NUM_TIMES As Integer = 3
Dim loopNum As Integer = 0
Do Until loopNum = NUM_TIMES
    loopNum = loopNum + 1
    System.Console.WriteLine("Strike " & loopNum)
Loop
```

1. How many times does this loop execute?

    _____

2. What is the output of this program?

    _____

3. Is the output different if you change the order of the statements in the body of the loop, so that loopNum = loopNum + 1 comes after the output statement?

    _____

4. What is the loop control variable?

    _____

 By revising the same file three different ways in this chapter, you have seen that a single problem can be solved in different ways.

 LAB 5.4   Using a Do Until Loop

In this lab, you work with the same Visual Basic program you worked with in Labs 5.1 and 5.3. As in those earlier labs, the completed program should print the numbers 0 through 10, along with their values doubled and quadrupled. However, in this lab you should accomplish this using a Do Until loop.

1. Open the source code file named NewestDoubleQuadruple.vb using Notepad or the text editor of your choice.

2. Write a Do Until loop that uses the loop control variable to take on the values 0 through 10.

3. In the body of the loop, calculate the double and the quadruple using the value of the loop control variable.

4. Save this source code file in a directory of your choice, and then make that directory your working directory.

5. Compile the source code file NewestDoubleQuadruple.vb.

6. Execute the program. Is the output the same as in Labs 5.1 and 5.3?

Nesting Loops

As the logic of your programs becomes more complex, you may find that you need to use nested loops. That is, you may need to include a loop within another loop. You have learned that when you use nested loops in a program, you must use multiple control variables to control the separate loops.

In Chapter 5 of *Programming Logic and Design, Sixth Edition*, you studied the design logic for a program that produces a quiz answer sheet. A section of the pseudocode for this program is as follows:

```
num PARTS = 5
num QUESTIONS = 3
string PART_LABEL = "Part "
sting LINE = ". _____"
string QUIT = "ZZZ"
output quizName
partCounter = 1
while partCounter <= PARTS
   output PART_LABEL, partCounter
   questionCounter = 1
   while questionCounter <= QUESTIONS
       output questionCounter, LINE
       questionCounter = questionCounter + 1
   endwhile
   partCounter = partCounter + 1
endwhile
output "Enter next quiz name or ", QUIT, " to quit"
input quizName
```

This pseudocode includes two loops. The outer loop uses the loop control variable `partCounter` to control the loop using the sentinel value, 5 (constant value of `PARTS`). The inner loop uses the control variable `questionCounter` to keep track of the number of lines to print for the questions in a part of the quiz. Refer to Chapter 5 in *Programming Logic and Design, Sixth Edition* for a line-by-line description of the pseudocode. When you are sure you understand the logic, take a look at the code sample that follows. This code sample shows some of the Visual Basic code for the Answer Sheet program.

```
Dim partCounter As Integer
Dim questionCounter As Integer
Const PARTS As Integer = 5
Const QUESTIONS As Integer = 3
Const PART_LABEL As String = "Part "
```

```
Const LINE As String = ". _____"
partCounter = 1
Do While partCounter <= PARTS
    System.Console.WriteLine(PART_LABEL & partCounter)
    questionCounter = 1
    Do While questionCounter <= QUESTIONS
        System.Console.WriteLine(questionCounter & LINE)
        questionCounter = questionCounter + 1
    Loop
    partCounter = partCounter + 1
Loop
```

The entire Visual Basic program is saved in a file named
AnswerSheet.vb. This file is included with the data files for this book.
You may want to study the source code, compile it, and execute the
program to experience how nested loops behave.

Exercise 5-6: Nesting Loops

In this exercise, you use what you have learned about nesting loops.
Study the following code, and then answer Questions 1–3.

```
Dim sum As Integer = 0
Const MAX_ROWS As Integer = 5
Const MAX_COLS As Integer = 4
Dim rows As Integer
Dim columns As Integer
For rows = 0 To MAX_ROWS
    For columns = 0 To MAX_COLS
        sum += rows + columns
    Next columns
Next rows
System.Console.WriteLine("Value of sum is " & sum)
```

1. How many times does the outer loop execute?

    _____

2. How many times does the inner loop execute?

    _____

3. What is the value of sum printed by
    System.Console.WriteLine()?

    _____

LAB 5.5   Nesting Loops

In this lab, you add nested loops to a Visual Basic program
provided with the data files for this book. The program
should print the outline of a rectangle, as shown in
Figure 5-2. The rectangle is printed using asterisks, four across and

six down. Note that this program uses `System.Console.Write("*")` to print an asterisk without a new line.

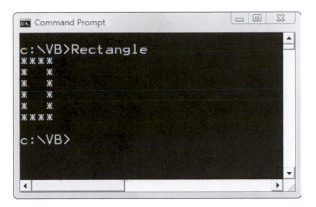

Figure 5-2 Rectangle printed by the Rectangle program

1. Open the source code file named `Rectangle.vb` using Notepad or the text editor of your choice.

2. Write the nested loops to control the number of rows and the number of columns that make up the rectangle.

3. In the loop body, use a nested `If` statement to decide when to print an asterisk and when to print a space. The output statements have been written, but you must decide when and where to use them.

4. Save this source code file in a directory of your choice, and then make that directory your working directory.

5. Compile the source code file `Rectangle.vb`.

6. Execute the program. Your rectangle outline should look like the rectangle outline in Figure 5-2.

7. Modify the program to change the number of rows from six to eight and the number of columns from four to 10. What does the rectangle look like now?

Accumulating Totals in a Loop

You can use a loop in Visual Basic to accumulate a total as your program executes. For example, assume that your computer science instructor has asked you to design and write a program that she can use to calculate an average score for the midterm exam she gave last week. To find the average test score, you need to add all the students' test scores, and then divide that sum by the number of students who took the midterm.

Note that the logic for this program should include a loop that will execute for each student in the class. In the loop, you get a student's test score as input and add that value to a total. After you get all of the test scores and accumulate the sum of all the test scores, you divide that sum by the number of students. You should plan to ask the user to input the number of student test scores that will be entered because your instructor wants to reuse this program using a different number of students each time it is executed.

As you review your work, you realize that the program will accumulate a sum within the loop and that you will also need to keep a count for the number of students. You learned in *Programming Logic and Design, Sixth Edition* that you add 1 to a counter each time a loop executes and that you add some other value to an accumulator. For this program, that other value added to the accumulator is a student's test score.

The following Visual Basic code sample shows the loop required for this program. Notice that the loop body includes an accumulator and a counter.

```
' Get user input to control loop
stringNum = InputBox$("Enter number of students: ")
' Convert number String to Integer
numStudents = Convert.ToInt32(stringNum)
' Initialize accumulator variable to 0
testTotal = 0
' Loop for each student
For stuCount = 1 To numStudents
    ' Input student test score
    stringScore = InputBox$("Enter student's score: ")
    ' Convert to Integer
    testScore = Convert.ToInt32(stringScore)
    ' Accumulate total of test scores
    testTotal += testScore
Next stuCount
' Calculate average test score
average = testTotal / numStudents
```

If `testTotal` is not initialized, it will automatically be assigned the value 0. However, it is considered a good programming practice to initialize variables.

In the code, you use the `InputBox$()` function to ask your user to tell you how many students took the test. Then the program converts the `String` value that is returned by the `InputBox$()` function to an `Integer` so that value can be used in arithmetic calculations. Next, the accumulator `testTotal` is initialized to 0.

After the accumulator is initialized, the code uses a `For` loop and the loop control variable `stuCount` to control the loop. A `For` loop is a good choice because, at this point in the program, you know how many times the loop should execute. You use the `For` loop to initialize `stuCount`, and then test to see if `stuCount` is less than or equal to numStudents. If the result of this comparison is True, the body of the loop executes, using the InputBox$() function again, this time asking the user to enter a test score.

As you examine the code, note that because the InputBox$() function returns the String version of the value entered by the user, the program must convert this String to an Integer by using the Convert.ToInt32() method. Then, you must add the value of testScore to the accumulator testTotal. The loop control variable stuCount is then incremented, and the incremented value is tested to see if it is less than or equal to numStudents. If this is True again, the loop executes a second time. The loop continues to execute until the value of stuCount is greater than numStudents. Outside the For loop, the program calculates the average test score by dividing testTotal by numStudents.

 Be sure to calculate the average outside of the loop, not inside the loop. The only way to calculate the average inside the loop is to do it each time the loop executes, but that is inefficient.

If a user entered 0, meaning 0 students took the midterm, the For loop would not execute because the value of numStudents is 0, and the value of stuCount is 1. Also, the statement following the loop average = testTotal / numStudents results in a Divide By 0 error because dividing by 0 is not allowed.

The entire Visual Basic program discussed in this section is saved in a file named TestAverage.vb. You may want to study the source code, compile it, and execute the program to experience how accumulators and counters behave.

Exercise 5-7: Accumulating Totals in a Loop

In this exercise, you use what you have learned about counters and accumulating totals in a loop. Study the Visual Basic code that follows, and then answer Questions 1–4. The complete program is saved in the file named Rainfall.vb. You may want to compile and execute the program to help you answer these questions.

```
Dim counter As Integer
Dim stringRain As String
Dim rainfall As Double
Dim sum As Double = 0.0
Dim average As Double
Const DAYS_IN_WEEK As Integer = 7
For counter = 1 To DAYS_IN_WEEK
    stringRain = InputBox$( _
               "Enter rainfall amount for Day " & counter)
    rainfall = Convert.ToDouble(stringRain)
    System.Console.WriteLine("Day " & counter & _
          " rainfall amount is "  & rainfall & " inches")
    sum += rainfall
Next counter
' calculate average
average = sum / DAYS_IN_WEEK
```

1. What happens when you compile this program if the variable `sum` is not initialized with the value 0?

   _____

2. Could you replace `sum += rainfall` with `sum = sum + rainfall`?

   _____

3. The variable `average` should be declared as what data type to calculate the most accurate average rainfall?

   _____

4. Could you replace `DAYS_IN_WEEK` in the statement `average = sum / DAYS_IN_WEEK` with the variable named `counter` and still get the desired result? Explain.

   _____

   _____

LAB 5.6 Accumulating Totals in a Loop

In this lab, you add a loop and the statements that make up the loop body to a Visual Basic program provided with the data files for this book. When completed, the program should calculate the total daily sales for a book store. Your loop should execute until the user enters the word "done" instead of a book title. After the user enters a book title, he or she should be asked to enter the transaction amount. The transaction amounts are listed in Table 5-1.

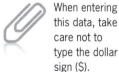

When entering this data, take care not to type the dollar sign ($).

Book Title	Transaction Amount ($)
The Lost Symbol	29.95
The Time Traveler's Wife	14.95
The Weight of Silence	13.95
The White Queen	25.99
My Life in France	15.00
Three Cups of Tea	15.00
Outliers	27.99

Table 5-1   Input for Lab 5.6

Note that variables have been declared for you, and the input and output statements have been written, but you must decide where they belong in the program.

1. Open the source code file named BookSales.vb using Notepad or the text editor of your choice.

2. Write a loop and a loop body that allows you to calculate a total of daily sales for the bookstore.

3. Save this source code file in a directory of your choice, and then make that directory your working directory.

4. Compile the source code file BookSales.vb.

5. Execute the program using the data listed in Table 5-1. Record the output of this program.

_____

_____

Using a Loop to Validate Input

In Chapter 5 of *Programming Logic and Design, Sixth Edition*, you learned that you cannot count on users to enter valid data in programs that ask them to enter data. You also learned that you should validate input from your user so you can avoid problems caused by invalid input.

If your program requires a user to enter a specific value—such as "Y" or "N"— in response to a question, then your program should validate that your user entered an exact match to either "Y" or "N". You must also decide what action to take in your program if the user's input is not either "Y" or "N". As an example of testing for an exact match, consider the following code:

```
Dim answer As String
answer = InputBox$( _ "Do you want to continue? Enter Y or N.")
Do While answer <> "Y" And answer <> "N"
    answer = InputBox$( _
            "Invalid Response. Please type Y or N.")
Loop
```

In the example, the variable named answer contains your user's answer to the question "Do you want to continue? Enter Y or N." In the Do While loop, the program compares the value of answer with "Y" and with "N" to see if your user really did enter a "Y" or an "N". If not, the program enters the loop, telling the user he or she entered invalid input and then requesting that he or she type a "Y" or an "N". The value of answer is tested again to see if the user entered valid data this time. If not, the loop body executes again and continues to execute until the user enters valid input.

You can also verify user input in a program that requests a user to enter numeric data. For example, your program could ask a user to enter a number in the range of 1 to 4. It is very important to verify this numeric input, especially if your program uses the input in arithmetic calculations. What would happen if the user entered the word "one" instead of the number 1? Or, what would happen if the user entered 100? More than likely, your program would not run correctly. The following code example illustrates how you can verify that a user enters correct numeric data:

```
Dim stringAnswer As String
Dim answer As Integer
Const MIN_NUM As Integer = 1
Const MAX_NUM As Integer = 4
stringAnswer = InputBox$( _
               "Please enter a number in the range of " & _
               MIN_NUM & " to " & MAX_NUM & ": ")
answer = Convert.ToInt32(stringAnswer)
Do While answer < MIN_NUM Or answer > MAX_NUM
   stringAnswer = InputBox$("Number must be between " & _
               MIN_NUM & " and " & MAX_NUM & _
               ". Please try again: ")
   answer = Convert.ToInt32(stringAnswer)
Loop
```

Exercise 5-8: Validating User Input

In this exercise, you use what you have learned about validating user input to answer Questions 1–4.

1. You plan to use the following statement in a Visual Basic program to validate user input:

    ```
    Do While inputString = ""
    ```

    What would your user enter to cause this test to be True?

    _____

2. You plan to use the following statement in a Visual Basic program to validate user input:

    ```
    Do While userAnswer = "N" Or userAnswer = "n"
    ```

    What would a user enter to cause this test to be True?

    _____

3. You plan to use the following statement in a Visual Basic program to validate user input:

    ```
    Do While userAnswer < 4 Or userAnswer > 10
    ```

    What would a user enter to cause this test to be True?

    _____

4. You plan to use the following statement in a Visual Basic program to validate user input:

```
Do While userAnswer < 6 And userAnswer > 12
```

What would a user enter to cause this test to be **True**?

LAB 5.7 Validating User Input

In this lab, you make additions to a Visual Basic program provided with the data files for this book. The program is a guessing game. A random number between 1 and 10 is generated in the program. The user enters a number between 1 and 10, trying to guess the correct number. If the user guesses correctly, the program congratulates the user, and then the loop that controls guessing numbers exits; otherwise the program asks the user if he or she wants to guess again. If the user enters "Y", he or she can guess again. If the user enters "N", the loop exits. You can see that the "Y" or "N" is the sentinel value that controls the loop. Note that the entire program has been written for you. You need to add code that validates correct input, which is "Y" or "N" when the user is asked if he or she wants to guess a number, and a number in the range of 1 through 10 when the user is asked to guess a number.

1. Open the source code file named GuessNumber.vb using Notepad or the text editor of your choice.

2. Write loops that validate input at all places in the code where the user is asked to provide input. Comments have been included in the code to help you identify where these loops should be written.

3. Save this source code file in a directory of your choice, and then make that directory your working directory.

4. Compile the source code file GuessNumber.vb.

5. Execute the program. See if you can guess the randomly generated number. Execute the program several times to see if the random number changes. Also, test the program to verify that incorrect input is handled correctly. On your best attempt, how many guesses did you have to take to guess the correct number?

Using Arrays in Visual Basic Programs

After studying this chapter, you will be able to:

- ◎ Use arrays in Visual Basic programs
- ◎ Search an array for a particular value
- ◎ Use parallel arrays in a Visual Basic program

You should do the exercises and labs in this chapter after you have finished Chapter 6 of your book, *Programming Logic and Design, Sixth Edition*. In this chapter, you learn how to use Visual Basic to declare and initialize arrays. You then access the elements of an array to assign values and process them within your program. You also learn why it is important to stay within the bounds of an array. In addition, you study some programs written in Visual Basic that implement the logic and design presented in *Programming Logic and Design, Sixth Edition*.

Array Basics

An **array** is a group of data items in which every item has the same data type, is referenced using the same variable name, and is stored in consecutive memory locations. To reference individual elements in an array, you use a subscript. Think of a **subscript** as the position number of a value within an array. In Visual Basic, subscript values begin with 0 (zero) and end with *n-1*, where *n* is the number of items stored in the array. You might be tempted to think that the first value in an array would be element number 1, but in fact it would be element number 0. The fifth element in an array would be element number 4.

To use an array in a Visual Basic program, you must learn how to declare an array, initialize an array with predetermined values, access array elements, and stay within the bounds of an array. In the next section you'll focus on declaring arrays.

Declaring Arrays

Before you can use an array in a Visual Basic program, you must first **declare** it. That is, you must give it a name and specify the data type for the data that will be stored in it. In some cases, you also specify the number of items that will be stored in the array. The following code shows one way to declare two arrays, one named `cityPopulations` that will be used to store three `Integers` and another named `cities` that will be used to store three `Strings`:

```
Dim cityPopulations(2) As Integer
Dim cities(2) As String
```

As shown, you begin with the keyword `Dim` followed by the name of the array. Following the array name, you place the upper bound of the array within parentheses. The **upper bound** is the subscript associated with the last element that may be stored in the array. Next comes the keyword As followed by the data type of the items that will be stored in the array. Remember in Visual Basic, the **lower bound** is 0 and the **upper bound** is *n-1*, where *n* is the number of items that may be stored in the array.

In this example, the two array declaration statements cause the Visual Basic compiler to allocate enough consecutive memory locations to store three elements of data type Integer for the array named cityPopulations and enough consecutive memory locations to store three elements of data type String for the cities array.

Initializing Arrays

In Visual Basic, array elements are automatically initialized to 0 (zero) for numeric data types, and Strings are automatically initialized to a null value. A **null value** is the 0 value for Strings and can be thought of as a value of "nothing." You can and will sometimes want to initialize arrays with values that you choose. This can be done when you declare the array. To initialize an array when you declare it, use curly braces to surround a comma-delimited list of data items, as shown in the following example:

```
Dim cityPopulations() As Integer = {9500000, 871100, 23900}
Dim cities() As String = {"Chicago","Detroit","Batavia"}
```

Alternatively, you can use assignment statements to provide values for array elements after an array is declared, as in the following example:

```
cityPopulations(0) = 9500000
cities(0) = "Chicago"
```

A loop is often used to assign values to the elements in an array, as shown here:

```
Dim loopIndex As Integer
For loopIndex = 0 To 2
   cityPopulations(loopIndex) = 12345
   cities(loopIndex) = "AnyCity"
Next loopIndex
```

The first time this loop is encountered, loopIndex is assigned the value 0. Because 0 is less than or equal to 2, the body of the loop executes, assigning the value 12345 to cityPopulations(0) and the value "AnyCity" to cities(0). Next, the value of loopIndex is incremented and takes on the value 1. Because 1 is less than or equal to 2, the loop executes a second time, and the value 12345 is assigned to cityPopulations(1), and "AnyCity" is assigned to cities(1). Each time the loop executes, the value of `loopIndex` is incremented. This allows you to access a different location in the arrays each time the body of the loop executes.

Accessing Array Elements

You need to access individual locations in an array when you assign a value to an array element, print its value, change its value, assign the value to another variable, and so forth. In Visual Basic, you use an integer expression placed in parentheses to indicate which element in the array you want to access. This integer expression is the subscript.

Remember that subscript values begin with 0 (zero) in Visual Basic.

The following Visual Basic program declares an array of data type `Double`, initializes an array of data type `Double`, copies values from one array to another, changes several values stored in the array named `target`, and prints the values of the arrays named `source` and `target`. You can compile and execute this program if you like. It is stored in the file named `ArrayTest.vb`.

Later in this chapter, you will learn how to use a named constant in an array declaration.

```vbnet
Option Explicit On
Option Strict On
Module ArrayTest
    Sub Main()
        Dim target(2) As Double
        Dim source() As Double = {1.0, 5.5, 7.9}
        Dim loopIndex As Integer
        ' Copy values from source to target
        For loopIndex = 0 to 2
            target(loopIndex) = source(loopIndex)
        Next loopIndex
        ' Assign values to two elements of target
        target(0) = 2.0
        target(1) = 4.5
        ' Print values stored in source and target arrays
        For loopIndex = 0 To 2
            System.Console.WriteLine("Source " & _
                                source(loopIndex))
            System.Console.WriteLine("Target " & _
                                target(loopIndex))
        Next loopIndex
    End Sub
End Module
```

Staying Within the Bounds of an Array

As a Visual Basic programmer, you must be careful to ensure that the subscript values you use to access array elements are within the legal bounds. When a program executes, Visual Basic checks to make sure that a subscript used in your program is greater than or equal to 0 and less than the length of the array. For example, suppose you declare an array named `numbers` as follows:

```
Dim numbers(9) As Integer
```

In this case, Visual Basic checks to make sure the subscripts you use to access this array are integer values between 0 and 9.

When using a loop to access array elements, be sure that the test you use to terminate the loop keeps you within the legal bounds, 0 to *n-1*, where *n* is the number of items that may be stored in the array.

If you access an array element that is not in the legal bounds, Visual Basic generates an `IndexOutOfRangeException`. Generally speaking, an **exception** is an error that occurs during program execution that disrupts the normal flow of the program and can cause your program to terminate abnormally.

For example, consider the highlighted number in the following code, which is taken from the previous Visual Basic program example:

```
Dim source() As Double = {1.0, 5.5, 7.9}
Dim loopIndex As Integer
For loopIndex = 0 To 2
```

If you change the highlighted value to 3, as shown here, your program will still compile with no errors:

```
For loopIndex = 0 To 3
```

A problem arises, however, when Visual Basic executes your program because the loop will execute when the value of `loopIndex` is 3. When you access the array element `source(3)`, you are outside the bounds of the array because there is no such element in this array. As shown in Figure 6-1, an `IndexOutOfRangeException` occurs, and your program terminates.

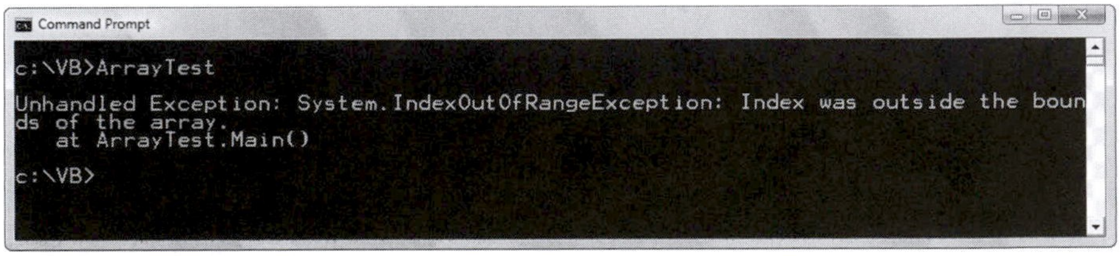

Figure 6-1   `IndexOutOfRangeException`

Using Constants with Arrays

It is a good programming practice to use a named constant to help you stay within the bounds of an array when you write programs that declare and access arrays. In Visual Basic, you can use a named constant that you create or you can use a constant that Visual Basic automatically creates for you to represent the array size.

The following example shows how to use a named constant that you create:

```
Const NUM_ITEMS As Integer = 3
Dim target(NUM_ITEMS - 1) As Double
Dim loopIndex As Integer
For loopIndex = 0 To NUM_ITEMS - 1
    target(loopIndex) = loopIndex + 10
Next loopIndex
```

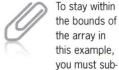

To stay within the bounds of the array in this example, you must subtract 1 from NUM_ITEMS.

In Visual Basic, after you declare the array named **target**, its size is automatically stored in a field named **target.Length**.

You can use this value in your Visual Basic programs, as shown in the following code sample. In this sample, the field **target.Length** is highlighted, so you can spot it easily.

```
Const NUM_ITEMS As Integer = 3
Dim target(NUM_ITEMS - 1) As Double
Dim loopIndex as Integer
For loopIndex = 0 To target.Length - 1
    target(loopIndex) = loopIndex + 10
Next loopIndex
```

Arrays are considered objects in Visual Basic, and **Length** is a property of the array.

When you use **Length**, a constant created by Visual Basic, to represent the size of an array, it is still a good programming practice to use a named constant when declaring an array. That way, if you must alter the code to change the array size, you only have to make the change in one location in your code.

To stay within the bounds of the array, you must subtract 1 from **target.Length**.

Exercise 6-1: Array Basics

In this exercise, you use what you have learned about declaring and initializing arrays to answer Questions 1–4.

1. Write array declarations for each of the following:

    a. Six book prices

    _____

    b. Three CD titles

    _____

    c. 15 whole numbers

    _____

2. Declare and initialize arrays that store the following:

    a. The ages 22, 34, 7, 62, and 52

    b. The names John, Laila, and Ed

    c. The prices 7.00, 95.00, and 174.50

3. Write an assignment statement that assigns the value 99 to the first element of an array of 20 integers named `miles`.

4. Write an assignment statement that assigns the value 99 to the last element of an array of 20 integers named `miles`.

102

LAB 6.1   Using Arrays

In this lab, you complete a partially prewritten Visual Basic program that uses an array. The program prompts the user to interactively enter 10 integer values, which the program stores in an array. It should then find the minimum and maximum values stored in the array, as well as the average of the 10 values. The data file provided for this lab includes the input statement and some variable declarations. Comments are included in the file to help you write the remainder of the program.

1. Open the source code file named `MinMax.vb` using Notepad or the text editor of your choice.

2. Write the Visual Basic statements as indicated by the comments.

3. Save this source code file in a directory of your choice, and then make that directory your working directory.

4. Compile the source code file `MinMax.vb`.

5. Execute the program using the following 10 values: 33, 12, -6, 1001, 57, -1, 999, 365, 921, and 724. The minimum value should be -6, and the maximum value should be 1001. The average should be 410.5.

Searching an Array for an Exact Match

One of the programs discussed in *Programming Logic and Design, Sixth Edition* uses an array to hold valid item numbers for a mail-order business. The idea is that when a customer orders an item, you can determine if the customer ordered a valid item number by searching through the array for that item number. This program relies on a technique called setting a flag to verify that an item exists in an array. The pseudocode and the Visual Basic code for this program are shown in Figure 6-2.

```
start
   Declarations
      num item
      num SIZE = 6
      num VALID_ITEM[SIZE] = 106, 108, 307,
         405, 457, 688
      num sub
      string foundIt
      num badItemCount = 0
      string MSG_YES = "Item available"
      string MSG_NO = "Item not found"
      num FINISH = 999
   getReady()
   while item <> FINISH
      findItem()
   endwhile
   finishUp()
stop

getReady()
   output "Enter item number or ", FINISH, " to quit"
   input item
return

findItem()
   foundIt = "N"
   sub = 0
   while sub < SIZE
      if item = VALID_ITEM[sub] then
         foundIt = "Y"
      endif
      sub = sub + 1
   endwhile
   if foundIt = "Y" then
      output MSG_YES
   else
      output MSG_NO
      badItemCount = badItemCount + 1
   endif
   output "Enter next item number or ", FINISH, " to quit"
   input item
return

finishUp()
  output badItemCount, " items had invalid numbers"
return
```

Figure 6-2 Pseudocode and Visual Basic code the for Mail Order program *(continues)*

(continued)

```
Option Explicit On
Option Strict On
Module MailOrder
    Sub Main()
        Dim item As Integer
        Dim badItemCount As Integer = 0
        Dim itemString As String
        Const SIZE As Integer = 6
        Dim VALID_ITEM() As Integer = {106, 108, 307, _
                                       405, 457, 688}

        Dim subscript As Integer
        Dim foundIt As Boolean = False
        Const MSG_YES As String = "Item Available"
        Const MSG_NO As String = "Item not found"
        Const FINISH As Integer = 999

        ' This is the work done in the getReady() procedure
        itemString = InputBox$("Enter item number: ")
        item = Convert.ToInt32(itemString)

        Do While item <> FINISH
            ' This is the work done in the findItem() procedure
            foundIt = False
            subscript = 0
            Do While subscript < SIZE
                If item = VALID_ITEM(subscript) Then
                    foundIt = True
                End If
                subscript = subscript + 1
            Loop
            If foundIt = True Then
                System.Console.WriteLine(MSG_YES)
            Else
                System. Console.WriteLine(MSG_NO)
                badItemCount = badItemCount + 1
            End If
            itemString = InputBox$( _
                        "Enter next item number or " & _
                        FINISH &  " to quit ")
            item = Convert.ToInt32(itemString)
        Loop
        ' This is the work done in the finishUp() procedure
        System.Console.WriteLine(badItemCount & _
                        " items had invalid numbers")
    End Sub
End Module
```

Figure 6-2   Pseudocode and Visual Basic code for the Mail Order program

As shown in Figure 6-2, when you translate the pseudocode to Visual Basic, you make a few changes. In both the pseudocode and the Visual Basic code, the variable named foundIt is the flag. However, in the Visual Basic code you assign the value False instead of the string constant "N" to the variable named foundIt. This is because the variable named foundIt is declared as a variable of the Boolean type. The Boolean data type is one of Visual Basic's primitive data types and is only used to store True and False values. Also, notice the pseudocode includes one statement to get the user's item number whereas it takes two statements in Visual Basic to get the user's input.

The program can be found in the file named MailOrder.vb.

Exercise 6-2: Searching an Array for an Exact Match

In this exercise, you use what you have learned about searching an array for an exact match. Study the following code, and then answer Questions 1–4. Note that this code may contain errors.

```
Dim states() As String = {"Illinois", "Ohio", _
                          "Iowa", "Texas"}
Dim saveIt As Integer
Dim i As Integer
Const MAX_STATES As Integer = 4
Dim inState As String
inState = InputBox$("Enter state name:")
For i = 0 To MAX_STATES
   If inState = states(i) Then
       saveIt = True
   End If
Next i
```

1. Is the For loop written correctly? If not, how can you fix it?

    _____

    _____

2. Which variable is the flag?

    _____

3. Is the flag variable declared correctly? If not, what should you do to fix it?

    _____

    _____

4. Is the comparison in the If statement done correctly?

    _____

LAB 6.2 Searching an Array for an Exact Match

In this lab, you use what you have learned about searching an array to find an exact match to complete a partially prewritten Visual Basic program. The program uses an array that contains valid area codes for 10 cities in the United States. You ask the user of the program to enter an area code; your program then searches the array for that area code. If it is not found, the program should print a message that informs the user that the area code is not found in the list of valid area codes.

The data file provided for this lab includes the input statements and the necessary variable declarations. You need to use a loop to examine all the items in the array and test for a match. You also need to set a flag if there is a match, and then test the flag variable to determine if the program should print the "Area code not found" message. Comments in the code tell you where to write your statements. You can use the Mail Order program in this chapter as a guide.

1. Open the source code file named **AreaCodes.vb** using Notepad or the text editor of your choice.

2. Study the prewritten code to make sure you understand it.

3. Write a loop statement that examines the area codes stored in the array.

4. Write code that tests for a match.

5. Write code that, when appropriate, prints the message: "Area code not found."

6. Save this source code file in a directory of your choice, and then make that directory your working directory.

7. Compile the source code file **AreaCodes.vb**.

8. Execute the program using the following as input:

   208
   219
   253
   630

Parallel Arrays

As you learned in *Programming Logic and Design, Sixth Edition*, you use parallel arrays to store values and to maintain a relationship between the items stored in the arrays. Figure 6-3 shows that the student ID number stored in `stuID(0)` and the grade stored in `grades(0)` are related—student 56 received a grade of 99.

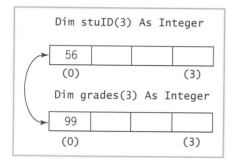

Figure 6-3   Parallel arrays

This relationship is established by using the same subscript value when accessing each array. Note that as the programmer, you must maintain this relationship in your code by always using the same subscript. Visual Basic does not create or maintain the relationship.

One of the programs discussed in *Programming Logic and Design, Sixth Edition* is an expanded version of the Mail Order program discussed in the "Searching an Array for an Exact Match" section earlier in this chapter. In the expanded program, you need to determine the price of the ordered item and print the item number along with the price. You use parallel arrays to help you organize the data for the program. One array, `VALID_ITEM`, contains six valid item numbers. The other array, `VALID_PRICE`, contains six valid prices. Each price is in the same position as the corresponding item number in the other array.

When a customer orders an item, you search the `VALID_ITEM` array for the customer's item number. When the item number is found, you use the price stored in the same location of the `VALID_PRICE` array and then output the item number and the price. The complete Visual Basic program is stored in the file named `MailOrder2.vb`. The pseudocode and Visual Basic code that search the `VALID_ITEM` array, use a price from the `VALID_PRICE` array, and then print the ordered item and its price are shown in Figure 6-4.

```
start
   Declarations
      num item
      num price
      num SIZE = 6
      num VALID_ITEM[SIZE] = 106, 108, 307,
         405, 457, 688
      num VALID_PRICE[SIZE] = 0.59, 0.99,
         4.50, 15.99, 17.50, 39.00
      num sub
      string foundIt
      num badItemCount = 0
      string MSG_YES = "Item available"
      string MSG_NO = "Item not found"
      num FINISH = 999
   getReady()
   while item <> FINISH
      findItem()
   endwhile
   finishUp()
stop

getReady()
   output "Enter item number or ", FINISH, " to quit"
   input item
return

findItem()
   foundIt = "N"
   sub = 0
   while sub < SIZE
      if item = VALID_ITEM[sub] then
         foundIt = "Y"
         price = VALID_PRICE[sub]
      endif
      sub = sub + 1
   endwhile
   if foundIt = "Y" then
      output MSG_YES
      output "The price of ", item, " is ", price
   else
      output MSG_NO
      badItemCount = badItemCount + 1
   endif
   output "Enter next item number or ", FINISH, " to quit"
   input item
return

finishUp()
   output badItemCount, " items had invalid numbers"
return
```

Figure 6-4 Pseudocode and Visual Basic code for the Mail Order 2 program
(continues)

(continued)

```
Option Explicit On
Option Strict On
Module MailOrder2
    Sub Main()
        Dim item As Integer
        Dim price As Double
        Dim badItemCount As Integer = 0
        Dim itemString As String
        Const SIZE As Integer = 6
        Dim VALID_ITEM() As Integer = {106, 108, 307, _
                                        405, 457, 688}
        Dim VALID_PRICE() As Double = {0.59, 0.99, 4.50, _
                                        15.99, 17.50, 39.00}
        Dim subscript As Integer
        Dim foundIt As Boolean = False
        Const MSG_YES As String = "Item Available"
        Const MSG_NO As String = "Item not found"
        Const FINISH As Integer = 999

        ' This is the work done in the getReady() procedure
        itemString = InputBox$("Enter item number: ")
        item = Convert.ToInt32(itemString)

        Do While item <> FINISH
            ' This is the work done in the findItem() procedure
            foundIt = False
            subscript = 0
            Do While subscript < SIZE
                If item = VALID_ITEM(subscript) Then
                    foundIt = True
                    price = VALID_PRICE(subscript)
                End If
                subscript = subscript + 1
            Loop
            If foundIt = True Then
                System.Console.WriteLine(MSG_YES)
                System.Console.WriteLine("The price of " & _
                                        item & " is " & price)
            Else
                System.Console.WriteLine(MSG_NO)
                badItemCount = badItemCount + 1
            End If
            itemString = InputBox$( _
                        "Enter next item number or " & _
                        FINISH & " to quit ")
            item = Convert.ToInt32(itemString)
        Loop
        ' This is the work done in the finishUp() procedure
        System.Console.WriteLine(badItemCount & _
                                " items had invalid numbers")
    End Sub
End Module
```

Figure 6-4 Pseudocode and Visual Basic code for the Mail Order 2 program

Exercise 6-3: Parallel Arrays

In this exercise, you use what you have learned about parallel arrays. Study the following code, and then answer Questions 1–4. Note that this code may contain errors.

```
Dim cities(4) As String = "Batavia", "Gary", "Elgin", "Troy"
Dim populations(4) As Integer = 23900, 102700, 24300, 5700
Const MAX_CITIES As Integer = 4
Dim saveIt As Integer
Dim foundIt As Boolean = False
Dim i As Integer
Dim inCity As String
inCity = InputBox$("Enter city name: ")
For i = 0 To MAX_CITIES
    If inCity = cities(i) Then
        saveIt = i
        foundIt = True
    End If
If foundIt = True Then
    System.Console.WriteLine("Population for " & _
            cities(saveIt) & " is " & populations(saveIt))
End If
```

1. Are the arrays declared and initialized correctly?

   _____

   If not, how can you fix them?

   _____

2. Is the For loop written correctly?

   _____

   If not, how can you fix it?

   _____

3. As written, how many times will the For loop execute?

   _____

4. How would you describe the purpose of the statement saveIt = i?

   _____

LAB 6.3 Parallel Arrays

In this lab, you use what you have learned about parallel arrays to complete a partially completed Visual Basic program. The program is described in Chapter 6 in *Programming Logic and Design, Sixth Edition*. The program should either print the name and price for a fast-food item from the Billy Goat Fast Food Restaurant or it should print the message: "Sorry, we do not carry that."

Read the problem description carefully before you begin. The data file provided for this lab includes the necessary variable declarations and input statements. You need to write the part of the program that searches for the name of the food item and either prints the name and price of the food item or prints the error message if the item is not found. Comments in the code tell you where to write your statements. You can use the Mail Order 2 program shown in Figure 6-4 as a guide.

1. Open the source code file named `BillyGoat.vb` using Notepad or the text editor of your choice.

2. Study the prewritten code to make sure you understand it.

3. Write the code that searches the array for the name of the food item ordered by the customer.

4. Write the code that prints the name and price of the food item or the error message.

5. Save this source code file in a directory of your choice, and then make that directory your working directory.

6. Compile the source code file `BillyGoat.vb`.

7. Execute the program using the following data, and record the output:

    Fries
    Pepsi
    Brat
    Pretzels
    Chips
    Coke
    Cheeseburger
    Hamburger

When evaluating data, Visual Basic distinguishes between uppercase letters and lowercase letters. This means, for example, that Pepsi is not the same as pepsi.

File Handling and Applications

After studying this chapter, you will be able to:

◎ Understand computer files

◎ Understand the data hierarchy

◎ Perform file operations

◎ Work with sequential files and control break logic

File Handling

Business applications are often required to manipulate large amounts of data that is stored in one or more files. As you learned in Chapter 7 of *Programming Logic and Design, Sixth Edition*, data is organized in a hierarchy. At the lowest level of the hierarchy is a **field**, which is a group of characters. On the next level up is a **record**, which is a group of related fields. For example, you could write a program that processes employee records, with each employee record consisting of three fields: the employee's first name, the employee's last name, and the employee's department number.

In Visual Basic, to use the data stored in a file, the program must first open the file and then read the data from the file. You use Visual Basic functions to accomplish this. In the next section, you learn how to open a file, close a file, read data from a file, and write data to a file.

Opening a File for Reading

To open a file and read data into a Visual Basic program, you use the `FileOpen()` function and specify the file number, the name of the file, and the mode. Look at the following example:

```
FileOpen(1, "inputFile.txt", OpenMode.Input)
```

In the example, notice the three data items that are enclosed in parentheses and separated by commas. These data items are called arguments. You will learn more about arguments in Chapter 9 of this book. The first argument is the file number, 1. In Visual Basic, each file used by a program must be associated with a number. Visual Basic allows programs to open up to 255 files as long as each file has its own unique file number, which can be an integer from 1 to 255. It is a Visual Basic convention that the first file opened uses the number 1.

You can use an `Integer` variable to store a file number, e.g.,
`Dim fileNumber As Integer = 1`.

The second argument is the name of the file to open, `inputFile.txt`, enclosed in double quotes. The third argument is the access mode, `OpenMode.Input`. Using `OpenMode.Input` opens a file for **read access**, which means that your program may now read data from the file.

Reading Data from an Input File

Once you have opened a file, you are ready to read the data in the file using the number associated with the file (not the file's name). The Input() function provides this capability.

The Input() function allows a program to read data from a file using a comma or a new line as a delimiter. A **delimiter** is defined as a character or combination of characters used to separate one item or set of data from another. For example, in comma-delimited records, a comma is used to separate each field of data.

We will assume that the input file for a program is organized so that an employee's first name, last name, and salary are on one line, delimited by commas, as follows:

Tim, Moriarty, 4000.00

To allow the program to read this data, you would write the following Visual Basic code:

```
FileOpen(1, "salary.dat", OpenMode.Input)
Dim firstName As String = ""
Dim lastName As String = ""
Dim salary As Double = 0.0
Input(1, firstName)
Input(1, lastName)
Input(1, salary)
FileClose(1)
```

If you omit the file number in the FileClose() function, all files that are currently open in your program will be closed.

The first line of the preceding code opens the file named salary.dat. The next three lines in the example declare and initialize two String variables named firstName and lastName, and the Double variable named salary. Next, the Input() function is used three times to read the three comma delimited items of input from the file associated with the number 1. After this code executes, the variable named firstName contains the value "Tim", the variable named lastName contains the value "Moriarty", and the variable named salary contains the value 4000.00. The last line, FileClose(1), closes the file having the file number 1. It is a good programming practice to close a file when you are finished using it in your program.

Reading Data Using a Loop and EOF

In a program that has to read large amounts of data, it is usually best to have the program use a loop. In the loop, the program continues to read from the file until the **End of File (EOF)** marker is encountered. The EOF marker is automatically placed at the end of a file when the file is saved. The EOF() function returns a True value when EOF is reached. The Visual Basic code that follows shows how to use the EOF() function as part of a loop:

```
Do While Not EOF(1)
     ' Read a record
Loop
```

In this example, the return value of the EOF() function is negated and then tested as part of the Do While loop. Notice the file number (1) within the parentheses of the EOF() function. The file number is used to instruct the EOF() function to check for EOF on the file associated with file number 1. As long as the negated value returned by the EOF() function is equal to True, the result is True, and the loop is entered. As soon as EOF is encountered, the test becomes False, and the program exits the loop.

Opening a File for Writing

To write data from a Visual Basic program to an output file, the program must first open a file. To open a file in Visual Basic to write data to it, you use the FileOpen() function and specify the file number, the name of the file, and the mode. Look at the following example:

```
FileOpen(2, "outputFile.txt", OpenMode.Output)
```

In the example, notice the three function arguments are enclosed in parentheses and separated by commas. The first argument is the file number, 2. In Visual Basic, each file used by a program must be associated with a number.

The second argument is the name of the file to open, outputFile.txt, enclosed in double quotes. The third argument is the access mode, OpenMode.Output. Using OpenMode.Output opens a file for **write access**, which means that your program may now write data to the file.

Opening a file for output is considered a **destructive process**. This means if the file you open for output already exists, all of the data it contains is destroyed.

Writing Data to an Output File

Once you have opened a file for output, the program is ready to write data to the file. You can use the Write() function to accomplish this.

As an example, assume that an employee's firstName, lastName, and salary have been read from an input file as in the previous example and that the employee is to receive a 15 percent salary increase that is calculated as follows:

```
Const INCREASE As Double = 1.15
Dim newSalary As Double
newSalary = salary * INCREASE
```

You now want to write the employee's firstName, lastName, and newSalary to the output file named newSalary2011.dat. The code that follows accomplishes this task:

```
FileOpen(2, "newSalary2011.dat", OpenMode.Output)
Write(2, firstName)
Write(2, lastName)
Write(2, newSalary)
FileClose(2)
```

The last line of code, FileClose(2), closes the output file associated with file number 2.

The Visual Basic code shown in Figure 7-1 implements the file input and output operations discussed in this section, and Figure 7-2 illustrates the relationship between file numbers and the physical file stored on disk.

```
Module FileInputOutput
    Sub Main()
        Dim firstName As String = ""
        Dim lastName As String = ""
        Dim salary As Double = 0.0
        Dim newSalary As Double
        ' Open input file
        FileOpen(1,"C:\VB\salary.dat",OpenMode.Input)
        ' Open output file
        FileOpen(2,"C:\VB\newSalary2011.dat",OpenMode.Output)
        ' Read records from file and test for EOF
        Do While Not EOF(1)
            Input(1, lastName)
            Input(1, firstName)
            Input(1, salary)
            newSalary = salary * 1.15
            ' Write records to file
            Write(2, lastName)
            Write(2, firstName)
            Write(2, newSalary)
        Loop
        FileClose(1)
        FileClose(2)
    End Sub
End Module
```

Figure 7-1 Reading and writing file data

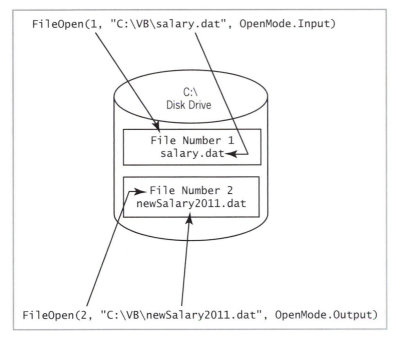

```
FileOpen(1, "C:\VB\salary.dat", OpenMode.Input)
```

C:\
Disk Drive

File Number 1
salary.dat

File Number 2
newSalary2011.dat

```
FileOpen(2, "C:\VB\newSalary2011.dat", OpenMode.Output)
```

Figure 7-2 Relationship between file numbers and physical files

Exercise 7-1: Opening Files and Performing File Input

In this exercise, you use what you have learned about opening a file and getting input into a program from a file. Study the following code, and then answer Questions 1–3.

```
1   FileOpen(1, myDvdFile.dat, OpenMode.Output)
2   Dim dvdName As String
3   Dim dvdPrice As String
4   Dim dvdShelf As String
5   Input(1,dvdName)
6   Input(1,dvdPrice)
7   Input(1,dvdShelf)
```

Figure 7-3 Code for Exercise 7-1

1. There are two errors on line 1. Describe the first error, and explain how to fix it.

   _____

2. Describe the second error on line 1, and explain how to fix it.

   _____

3. Assuming the errors in line 1 are corrected, consider the following data from the input file myDvdFile.dat:

   Lost, 35.00, 1A

   Watchmen, 29.00, 2C

   Heroes, 39.00, 3B

   a. What value is stored in the variable named dvdName?

      _____

   b. What value is stored in the variable name dvdPrice?

      _____

   c. What value is stored in the variable named dvdShelf?

      _____

LAB 7.1   Using an Input File

In this lab, you open a file and read input from that file in a prewritten Visual Basic program. The program should read and print the names of fish that are stored in the input file named fish.dat.

1. Open the source code file named Fish.vb using Notepad or the text editor of your choice.

2. Declare the variables you will need.

3. Write the Visual Basic statements that will open the input file fish.dat for reading.

4. Write a Do While loop to read the input until EOF is reached.

5. In the body of the loop, print the name of each fish on the user's screen.

6. Close the input file.

7. Save this source code file in a directory of your choice, and then make that directory your working directory.

8. Compile the source code file named `Fish.vb`.

9. Execute the program.

Understanding Sequential Files and Control Break Logic

As you learned in Chapter 7 of *Programming Logic and Design, Sixth Edition*, a **sequential file** is a file in which records are stored one after another in some order. The records in a sequential file are organized based on the contents of one or more fields, such as ID numbers, part numbers, or last names.

A **single-level control break** program reads data from a sequential file and causes a break in the logic based on the value of a single variable. In Chapter 7 of *Programming Logic and Design, Sixth Edition*, you learned about techniques you can employ to implement a single-level control break program. Be sure you understand these techniques before you continue with this chapter. The program described in Chapter 7 of *Programming Logic and Design, Sixth Edition* that produces a report of customers by state is an example of a single-level control break program. This program reads a record for each client, keeps a count of the number of clients in each state, and prints a report. As shown in Figure 7-4, the report generated by this program includes clients' names, cities, and states, along with a count of the number of clients in each state.

Company Clients by State of Residence			
Name	City	State	
Albertson	Birmingham	Alabama	
Davis	Birmingham	Alabama	
Lawrence	Montgomery	Alabama	
		Count for Alabama	3
Smith	Anchorage	Alaska	
Young	Anchorage	Alaska	
Davis	Fairbanks	Alaska	
Mitchell	Juneau	Alaska	
Zimmer	Juneau	Alaska	
		Count for Alaska	5
Edwards	Phoenix	Arizona	
		Count for Arizona	1

Figure 7-4 Control break report with totals after each state

Each client record is made up of the following fields: Name, City, and State. Note the following example records, each made up of three lines:

Albertson
Birmingham
Alabama
Lawrence
Montgomery
Alabama
Smith
Anchorage
Alaska

Remember that input records for a control break program are usually stored in a data file on a storage device, such as a disk, and the records are sorted according to a predetermined control break variable. For example, the control break variable for this program is state, so the input records would be sorted according to state.

Figure 7-5 includes the pseudocode for the Client By State program, and Figure 7-6 shows the Visual Basic code that implements the program.

```
start
   Declarations
      InputFile inFile
      string TITLE = "Company Clients by State of Residence"
      string COL_HEADS = "Name    City    State"
      string name
      string city
      string state
      num count = 0
      String oldState
   getReady()
   while not eof
      produceReport()
   endwhile
   finishUp()
stop

getReady()
   output TITLE
   output COL_HEADS
   open inFile "ClientsByState.dat"
   input name, city, state from inFile
   oldState = state
return
```

Figure 7-5 Client By State program pseudocode *(continues)*

(continued)

```
produceReport()
   if state <> oldState then
      controlBreak()
   endif
   output name, city, state
   count = count + 1
   input name, city, state from inFile
return

controlBreak()
   output "Count for ", oldState, count
   count = 0
   oldState = state
return

finishUp()
   output "Count for ", oldState, count
   close inFile
return
```

Figure 7-5   Client By State program pseudocode

```
1  ' ClientByState.vb - This program creates a report that
2  ' lists clients with a count of the number of clients for
3  ' each state.
4  ' Input:  client.dat
5  ' Output:  Report
6  Option Explicit On
7  Option Strict On
8  Module ClientByState
9     Sub Main()
10       ' Declarations
11       Const TITLE As String = vbNewLine & _
12        "Company Clients by State of Residence " & vbNewLine
13       Dim name As String = ""
14       Dim city As String  = ""
15       Dim state As String = ""
16       Dim count As Integer = 0
17       Dim oldState As String = ""
18       Dim done As Boolean
19
20       ' Work done in the getReady() procedure
21       FileOpen(1, "client.dat", OpenMode.Input)
22       System.Console.WriteLine(TITLE)
23       If Not EOF(1) Then
24          Input(1, name)
```

Figure 7-6   Client By State program written in Visual Basic *(continues)*

(continued)

```
25          Input(1, city)
26          Input (1, state)
27          done = False
28          oldState = state
29      Else
30          done = True
31      End If
32      Do While done = False
33          ' Work done in the produceReport() procedure
34          If state <> oldState Then
35              ' Work done in the controlBreak() procedure
36              System.Console.WriteLine(vbTab & vbTab & _
37              vbTab & "Count for " & oldState & " " & count)
38              count = 0
39              oldState = state
40          End If
41          System.Console.WriteLine(name & " " & city & _
42                                    " " & state)
43          count = count + 1
44          If Not EOF(1) Then
45              Input(1, name)
46              Input(1, city)
47              Input (1, state)
48              done = False
49          Else
50              done = True
51          End If
52      Loop
53      ' Work done in the finishUp() procedure
54      System.Console.WriteLine(vbTab & vbTab & vbTab & _
55          "Count for " & oldState & " " & count)
56      FileClose(1)
57   End Sub ' End of Main() procedure
58 End Module ' End of ClientByState Module
```

Figure 7-6   Client By State program written in Visual Basic

As you can see in Figure 7-6, the Visual Basic program begins on line 1 with comments that describe what the program does. (The line numbers shown in this program are not part of the Visual Basic code. They are included for reference only.) The program also includes comments that describe the program's input and output. Next comes the Visual Basic code that defines the ClientByState Module (line 8) and, within the Module, the Main() procedure (line 9).

Within the Main() procedure, lines 11 through 18 declare variables and constants and initialize them when appropriate. Lines 21 through 31 include the work done in the getReady() procedure, which includes opening the input file named `client.dat`, printing the heading for the report this program generates, and performing a priming read. You learned about performing a priming read in Chapter 3 of this book and in Chapter 3 of *Programming Logic and Design, Sixth Edition*.

Notice that the Visual Basic code in the priming read (lines 23 through 31) is a little different than the pseudocode. An `If` statement is used on line 23 to test if EOF was encountered. If EOF is not encountered, the result of this test will be `True`, causing the execution of the input statements that read the `name`, `city`, and `state` from the input file. The `Boolean` value `False` is also assigned to the variable named `done` on line 27 followed by assigning the current value of `state` to the variable named `oldState` on line 28. Remember that the variable `state` serves as the control break variable. If EOF is encountered, the result of this test will be `False`, causing the `Boolean` value `True` to be assigned to the variable named `done` on line 30. The `Boolean` variable named `done` is used later in the program to control the `Do While` loop.

Next comes the `Do While` loop (line 32), which continues to execute as long as the value of the `Boolean` variable `done` is `False`. The body of the `Do While` loop contains the work done in the `produceReport()` procedure. First, on line 34, an `If` statement tests the value of the control break variable, `state`, with the value of the variable named `oldState` to determine if the record the program is currently working with has the same state as the previous record's state. If it does not, this indicates the beginning of a new state. As a result, the program performs the work done in the `controlBreak()` procedure (lines 36 through 39). The work of the `controlBreak()` procedure does the following:

1. Prints the value of the variable named `count` that contains the count of clients in the current state (line 36 and 37).

2. Assigns the value 0 to the variable named `count` to prepare for the next state.

3. Assigns the value of the variable named `state` to the variable named `oldState` to prepare for the next state.

If the record the program is currently working with has the same state as the previous record's state, the `controlBreak()` procedure's work is not performed. Whether or not the current record's state is the same state as the previous record's state, the next statement to execute (line 41 and 42) prints the client's name, city, and state. Then the variable named `count` is incremented on line 43 followed by the program reading the next client's record on lines 44 through 51 using the same technique as the priming read.

The condition in the `Do While` loop on line 32 is then tested again, causing the loop to continue executing until the value of the variable named **done** is `True`. The variable named **done** is assigned the value `True` when the program encounters EOF when reading from the input file on line 50.

When the `Do While` loop is exited, the last section of the program executes. This consists of the work done in the `finishUp()` procedure and consists of:

- Printing the value of the variable named **count** (which is the count of the clients in the last state in the input file) on line 54 and 55.

- Closing the input file (line 56).

Exercise 7-2: Accumulating Totals in Single-Level Control Break Programs

In this exercise, you use what you have learned about accumulating totals in a single-level control break program. Study the following code, and then answer Questions 1–4.

```
If partNum <> oldPartNum Then
    System.Console.WriteLine("Part Number " & oldPartNum)
    totalParts = partNum
    oldPartNum = partNum
End If
```

1. What is the control break variable?

   _____

2. True or False? The value of the control break variable should never be changed.

   _____

3. Is `totalParts` being calculated correctly?

   _____

   If not, how can you fix the code?

   _____

4. True or False? In a control break program, it doesn't matter if the records in the input file are in a specified order.

   _____

LAB 7.2 Accumulating Totals in Single-Level Control Break Programs

In this lab, you will use what you have learned about accumulating totals in a single-level control break program to complete a Visual Basic program. The program should produce a report for a fast food restaurant owner to help her keep track of the hours worked by her part-time employees. The report should include the day of the week, the number of hours worked by each employee for each day, and the total hours worked by all employees each day. The report should look similar to the one shown in Figure 7-7.

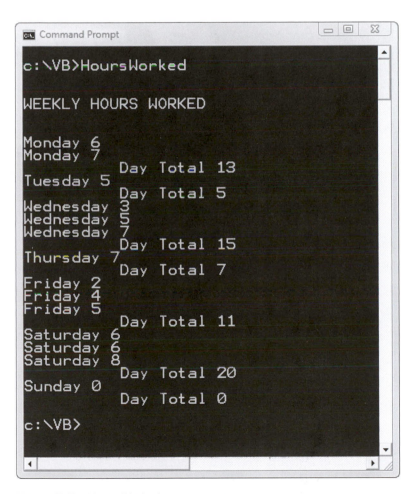

Figure 7-7   Hours Worked program report

The student file provided for this lab includes the necessary variable declarations and input and output statements. You need to implement the code that recognizes when a control break should occur. You also need to complete the control break code. Be sure to accumulate the daily totals for all days in the week. Comments in the code tell you where to write your code. You can use the **Client By State** program in this chapter as a guide for this new program.

1. Open the source code file named `HoursWorked.vb` using Notepad or the text editor of your choice.

2. Study the prewritten code to understand what has already been done.

3. Write the control break code in the `Main()` procedure.

4. Write the `dayChange()` control break code.

5. Save this source code file in a directory of your choice, and then make that directory your working directory.

6. Compile the source code file, `HoursWorked.vb`.

7. Execute this program using the following input values:

   Monday – 6 hours (employee 1), 7 hours (employee 2)
   Tuesday – 5 hours (employee 1)
   Wednesday – 3 hours (employee 1), 5 hours (employee 2), 7 hours (employee 3)
   Thursday – 7 hours (employee 1)
   Friday – 2 hours (employee 1), 4 hours (employee 2), 5 hours (employee 3)
   Saturday – 6 hours (employee 1), 6 hours (employee 2), 8 hours (employee 3)
   Sunday – 0 hours

   The program results should include:

   A total of 13 hours worked on Monday.
   A total of 5 hours worked on Tuesday.
   A total of 15 hours worked on Wednesday.
   A total of 7 hours worked on Thursday.
   A total of 11 hours worked on Friday.
   A total of 20 hours worked on Saturday.
   A total of 0 hours worked on Sunday.

Advanced Array Techniques

After studying this chapter, you will be able to:

- ◎ Explain the need to sort data
- ◎ Swap data values in a program
- ◎ Create a bubble sort in Visual Basic
- ◎ Work with multidimensional arrays

In this chapter, you review why you might want to sort data, how to use Visual Basic to swap two data values in a program, how to create a bubble sort in a Visual Basic program, and how to use multidimensional arrays. You should do the exercises and labs in this chapter after you have finished Chapter 8 in *Programming Logic and Design, Sixth Edition*.

Sorting Data

Data records are always stored in some order, but they may not be in the order in which you want to process or view them in your program. When this is the case, you need to give your program the ability to arrange (sort) records in a useful order. For example, the inventory records you need to process might be stored in product number order, but you might need to produce a report that lists products from lowest cost to highest cost. That means your program needs to be able to sort the records by cost.

Sorting makes searching for records easier and more efficient. A human can usually find what she is searching for by simply glancing through a group of data items, but a program must look through a group of data items one by one, making a decision about each one. When searching unsorted records for a particular data value, a program must examine every single record until it either locates the data value or determines that it does not exist. However, when searching sorted records, the program can quickly determine when to stop searching, as shown in the following step-by-step scenario:

1. The records used by your program are sorted by product number.

2. The user is searching for the product number 12367.

3. The program locates the record for product number 12368 but has not yet found product number 12367.

4. The program determines that the record for product number 12367 does not exist and, therefore, stops searching through the list.

Many search algorithms require that data be sorted before it can be searched. (An **algorithm** is a plan for solving a problem.) You can choose from many algorithms for sorting and searching for data. In *Programming Logic and Design, Sixth Edition*, you learned how to swap data values in an array, and you also learned about the bubble sort. Both of these topics are covered in this book.

Swapping Data Values

When you swap values, you place the value stored in one variable into a second variable, and then you place the value that was originally stored in the second variable in the first variable. You must also create a third variable to temporarily hold one of the values you want to swap so that a value is not lost. For example, if you try to swap values using the following code, you will lose the value of `score2`.

```
Dim score1 As Integer = 90
Dim score2 As Integer = 85
score2 = score1 ' The value of score2 is now 90.
score1 = score2 ' The value of score1 is also 90.
```

However, if you use a variable to temporarily hold one of the values, the swap is successful. This is shown in the following code.

```
Dim score1 As Integer = 90
Dim score2 As Integer = 85
Dim temp As Integer
temp = score2 ' The value of temp is 85.
score2 = score1 ' The value of score2 is 90.
score1 = temp ' The value of score1 is 85.
```

Exercise 8-1: Swapping Values

In this exercise, you use what you have learned about swapping values to answer the following question.

1. Suppose you have declared and initialized two `String` variables, `name1` and `name2`, in a Visual Basic program. Now, you want to swap the values stored in `name1` and `name2`, but only if the value of `name1` is greater than the value of `name2`.

   Write the Visual Basic code that accomplishes this task. The declarations are as follows:

   ```
   Dim name1 As String = "Smith"
   Dim name2 As String = "Smythe"
   ```

   _____

   _____

   _____

   _____

LAB 8.1   Swapping Values

In this lab, you will complete a Visual Basic program that swaps values stored in three `Integer` variables and determines maximum and minimum values. The Visual Basic file provided for this lab contains the necessary variable declarations, as well as the input and output statements. You want to end up with the smallest value stored in the variable named `value1` and the largest value stored in the variable named `value3`. You need to write the statements that compare the values and swap them if appropriate. Comments included in the code tell you where to write your statements.

1. Open the source code file named `Swap.vb` using the text editor of your choice.

2. Write the statements that test the first two integers, and swap them if necessary.

3. Write the statements that test the second and third integer, and swap them if necessary.

4. Write the statements that test the first and second integers again, and swap them if necessary.

5. Save this source code file in a directory of your choice, and then make that directory your working directory.

6. Compile the source code file, `Swap.vb`.

7. Execute the program using the following sets of input values, and record the output.

   255 313 –10

   610 993 37

   33 55 33

Using a Bubble Sort

A bubble sort is one of the easiest sorting techniques to understand. However, while it is logically simple, it is not very efficient. If the list contains *n* values, the bubble sort will make *n* – *1* passes over the list. For example, if the list contains 100 values, the bubble sort will make 99 passes over the data. During each pass, it examines successive overlapped pairs and swaps or exchanges those values that are out of order. After one pass over the data, the heaviest (largest) value sinks to the bottom and is then in the correct position in the list.

In *Programming Logic and Design, Sixth Edition*, you learned several ways to refine the bubble sort. One way is to reduce unnecessary comparisons by ignoring the last value in the list in the second pass through the data, because you can be sure it is already positioned correctly. On the third pass, you can ignore the last two values in the list because you know they are already positioned correctly. Thus, in each pass, you can reduce the number of items to be compared, and possibly swapped, by one.

Another refinement to the bubble sort is to eliminate unnecessary passes over the data in the list. When items in the array to be sorted are not entirely out of order, it may not be necessary to make *n – 1* passes over the data because after several passes, the items may already be in order. You can add a flag variable to the bubble sort, and then test the value of that flag variable to determine whether any swaps have been made in any single pass over the data. If no swaps have been made, you know that the list is in order; therefore, you do not need to continue with additional passes.

You also learned about using a constant for the size of the array to make your logic easier to understand and your programs easier to change and maintain. Finally, you learned how to sort a list of varying size by counting the number of items placed in the array as you read in items.

All of these refinements are included in the pseudocode for the Score Sorting program in Figure 8-1. The Visual Basic code that implements the Score Sorting logic is provided in Figure 8-2. The line numbers shown in Figure 8-2 are not part of the Visual Basic code. They are provided for reference only.

```
start
    num SIZE = 100
    num score[SIZE]
    num x
    num y
    num temp
    num numberOfEls = 0
    num comparisons
    num QUIT = 999
    String didSwap
    fillArray()
```

Figure 8-1   Pseudocode for Score Sorting program *(continues)*

(continued)

```
      sortArray()
      displayArray()
   stop

   num fillArray()
      x = 0
      output "Enter a score or ", QUIT, " to quit "
      input score[x]
      x = x + 1
      while x < SIZE AND score[x] <> QUIT
         output "Enter a score or ", QUIT, " to quit "
         input score[x]
         x = x + 1
      endwhile
      numberOfEls = x
      comparisons = numberOfEls - 1
   return

   void sortArray()
      x = 0
      didSwap = "Yes"
      while didSwap = "Yes"
         x = 0
         didSwap = "No"
         while x < comparisons
            if score[x] > score[x + 1] then
               swap()
               didSwap = "Yes"
            endif
            x = x + 1
         endwhile
         comparisons = comparisons - 1
      endwhile
   return

   void swap()
      temp = score[x + 1]
      score[x + 1] = score[x]
      score[x] = temp
   return

   void displayArray()
      x = 0
      while x < numberOfEls
         output score[x]
         x = x + 1
      endwhile
   return
```

Figure 8-1   Pseudocode for Score Sorting program

```
 1 ' StudentScores.vb - This program interactively reads a
 2 ' variable number of student test scores, stores the scores
 3 ' in an array, then sorts the scores in ascending order.
 4 ' Input:   Interactive
 5 ' Output:  Sorted list of student scores.
 6
 7 Option Explicit On
 8 Option Strict On
 9 Module StudentScores
10     Sub Main()
11         ' Declare variables.
12         ' Maximum size of array
13         Const SIZE As Integer = 100
14         Dim stuScoreString As String
15         ' Array of student scores.
16         Dim score(SIZE) As Integer
17         Dim x As Integer
18         Dim temp As Integer
19         ' Actual number of elements in array.
20         Dim numberOfEls As Integer = 0
21         Dim comparisons As Integer
22         Const QUIT As Integer = 999
23         Dim didSwap As Boolean
24
25         ' Work done in the fillArray procedure
26         x = 0
27         stuScoreString = InputBox$("Enter a score or " & _
28                         QUIT & " to quit ")
29         score(x) = Convert.ToInt32(stuScoreString)
30         x = x + 1
31         Do While x < SIZE And score(x - 1) <> QUIT
32            stuScoreString = InputBox$("Enter a score or " _
33                            & QUIT & " to quit ")
34            score(x) = Convert.ToInt32(stuScoreString)
35            x = x + 1
36         Loop  ' End of input loop.
37         numberOfEls = x - 1
38         comparisons = numberOfEls - 1
39
40         ' Work done in the sortArray() procedure
41         didSwap = True ' Set flag to true.
42         ' Outer loop controls number of passes over data.
43         Do While didSwap = True ' Test flag.
44             x = 0
45             didSwap = False
46             ' Inner loop controls number of items to compare.
47             Do While x < comparisons
48                If score(x) > score(x + 1) ' Swap?
49                    ' Work done in the swap() procedure
50                    temp = score(x + 1)
51                    score(x + 1) = score(x)
```

Figure 8-2 Visual Basic code for Score Sorting program *(continues)*

(continued)

```
52                    score(x) = temp
53                    didSwap = True
54                End If
55                x = x + 1 ' Get ready for next pair.
56            Loop
57            comparisons = comparisons - 1
58        Loop
59
60        ' Work done in the displayArray() procedure
61        x = 0
62        Do While x < numberOfEls
63            System.Console.WriteLine(score(x))
64            x = x + 1
65        Loop
66    End Sub ' End of Main() procedure.
67 End Module ' End of StudentScores module.
```

Figure 8-2   Visual Basic code for Score Sorting program

The Main() Procedure

As shown in Figure 8-2, the Main() procedure (line 10) declares variables and performs the work of the program. The variables include:

- A constant named SIZE, initialized with the value 100, which represents the maximum number of items this program can sort

- A String variable named stuScoreString that is used to hold the String version of a student score

- An array of data type Integer named score that is used to store up to a maximum of SIZE (100) items to be sorted

- An Integer variable named x that is used as the array subscript

- An Integer variable named temp that is used to swap the values stored in the array

- An Integer named numberOfEls that is used to hold the actual number of items stored in the array

- An Integer named comparisons that is used to control the number of comparisons that should be done

- An Integer constant named QUIT, initialized to 999, that is used to control the While loop

- A Boolean named didSwap that is used as a flag to indicate when a swap has taken place.

After these variables are declared, the work done in the fillArray() procedure begins on line 25. The fillArray() work is responsible for filling up the array with items to be sorted. On line 40, the work done in the sortArray() procedure begins. This work is responsible for sorting the items stored in the score array. Lastly, the work done in the diplayArray() procedure begins on line 60 and is responsible for displaying the sorted scores on the user's screen.

The fillArray() Procedure

The work done in the fillArray() procedure, which begins on line 25 in Figure 8-2, is responsible for: 1) storing the data in the array and 2) counting the actual number of elements placed in the array. The fillArray() procedure assigns the value 0 to the variable named x and then performs a priming read (lines 27 and 28) to retrieve the first student score from the user and stores the score in the String variable named stuScoreString. The String version of a student's score, stuScoreString, is then converted to an Integer and stored in the array named score at location x on line 29. Notice that the array subscript variable x is initialized to 0 on line 26 because the first position in an array is position 0. Also, notice that 1 is added to the variable named x on line 30 because x is used to count the number of scores entered by the user of the program.

On line 31, the condition that controls the Do While loop is tested. The Do While loop executes as long as the number of scores input by the user (represented by the variable named x) is less than SIZE (100) and as long as the user has not entered 999 (the value of the constant QUIT) for the student score. If x is less than SIZE and the user does not want to quit, there is enough room in the array to store the student score. In that case, the program retrieves the next student score, stores the score in the String variable named stuScoreString, converts the String to an Integer, and then stores the score in the array named score at location x on line 34. The program then adds 1 to the value of x (line 35) to get ready to store the next student score in the array. The loop continues to execute until the user enters the value 999 or until there is no more room in the array.

When the program exits the loop, the value of x $-$ 1 is assigned to the variable named numberOfEls on line 37. Notice that x is used as the array subscript and that its value is incremented every time the Do While loop executes, including when the user enters the value 999 in order to quit; therefore, x represents the number of student scores the user entered *plus one*. On line 38 the value of numberOfEls $-$ 1 is assigned to the variable named comparisons and represents the maximum number of elements the bubble sort will compare on a pass over the data stored in the array. It ensures that the program does not attempt to compare item x with item x + 1, when x is the last item in the array.

The `sortArray()` Procedure

The work done in the `sortArray()` procedure begins on line 40 and uses a refined bubble sort to rearrange the student scores in the array named `score` to be in ascending order. Refer to Figure 8-1, which includes the pseudocode, and Figure 8-2, which includes the Visual Basic code that implements the `sortArray()` procedure.

Line 41 initializes the flag variable `didSwap` to `True`, because, at this point in the program, it is assumed that items will need to be swapped.

The outer loop (line 43), `Do While didSwap = True`, controls the number of passes over the data. This logic implements one of the refinements discussed earlier—eliminating unnecessary passes over the data. As long as `didSwap` is `True`, the program knows that swaps have been made and that, therefore, the data is still out of order. Thus, when `didSwap` is `True`, the program enters the loop. The first statement in the body of the loop (line 44) is `x = 0`. The program assigns the value 0 to x because x is used as the array subscript. Recall that in Visual Basic, the first subscript in an array is number 0.

Next, to prepare for comparing the elements in the array, line 45 assigns the value `False` to `didSwap`. This is necessary because the program has not yet swapped any values in the array on this pass. The inner loop begins on line 47. The test, `x < comparisons`, controls the number of pairs of values in the array the program compares on one pass over the data. This implements another of the refinements discussed earlier—reducing unnecessary comparisons. The last statement in the outer loop (line 57), `comparisons = comparisons - 1`, subtracts 1 from the value of `comparisons` each time the outer loop executes. The program decrements `comparisons` because, when a complete pass is made over the data, it knows an item is positioned in the array correctly. Comparing the value of `comparisons` with the value of x in the inner loop reduces the number of necessary comparisons made when this loop executes.

On line 48, within the inner loop, adjacent items in the array are accessed and compared using the subscript variable x and x + 1. The adjacent array items are compared to see if the program should swap them. If the values should be swapped, the program executes the statements that make up the work done in the `swap()` procedure on lines 50 through 52, which uses the technique discussed earlier to rearrange the two values in the array. Next, line 53 assigns True to the variable named didSwap. The last task performed by the inner loop (line 55) is adding 1 to the value of the subscript variable x. This ensures that the next time through the inner loop, the program will compare the next two adjacent items in the array. The program continues to compare two adjacent items and possibly swap them as long as the value of x is less than the value of comparisons.

The displayArray() Procedure

In the displayArray() procedure, you print the sorted array on the user's screen. Figure 8-1 shows the pseudocode for this method. The Visual Basic code is shown in Figure 8-2.

The work done in the displayArray() procedure begins on line 60 of Figure 8-2. Line 61 assigns the value 0 to the subscript variable, x. This is done before the Do While loop is entered because the first item stored in the array is referenced using the subscript value 0. The loop in lines 62 through 65 prints all of the values in the array named score by adding 1 to the value of the subscript variable, x, each time the loop body executes. When the loop exits, the program ends.

Exercise 8-2: Using a Bubble Sort

In this exercise, you use what you have learned about sorting data using a bubble sort. Study the following code, and then answer Questions 1–4.

```
Dim numbers() As Integer = _
            {-6, 448, -20, 818, 42, 40, 320, 34}
Const NUM_ITEMS As Integer = 8
Dim j As Integer = 0
Dim k As Integer = 0
Dim temp As Integer = 0
Dim numPasses As Integer = 0
Dim numCompares As Integer = 0
Dim numSwaps As Integer = 0
Do While j < NUM_ITEMS - 1
   numPasses += 1
   Do While k < NUM_ITEMS - 1
      numCompares += 1
      If numbers(k) > numbers(k + 1) Then
         numSwaps += 1
         temp = numbers(k + 1)
         numbers(k + 1) = numbers(k)
         numbers(k) = temp
      End If
   Loop
Loop
```

1. Does this code perform an ascending sort or a descending sort? How do you know?

   _____

2. How many passes are made over the data in the array?

   _____

3. How many comparisons are made?

   _____

4. Do the variables named numPasses, numCompares, and numSwaps accurately keep track of the number of passes, compares, and swaps made in this bubble sort? Explain your answer.

   _____

LAB 8.2 Using a Bubble Sort

In this lab, you will complete a Visual Basic program that uses an array to store data for a computer science teacher. The program is similar to the program described in Chapter 8, Exercise 3 in *Programming Logic and Design, Sixth Edition*. The program should allow the user to enter a student's name and 10 quiz scores. The program should output the student's name and his or her eight highest quiz scores. The file provided for this lab contains the necessary variable declarations and input statements. You need to write the code that sorts the scores in ascending order using a bubble sort, and then prints the student's name and eight highest quiz scores. Comments in the code tell you where to write your statements.

1. Open the source code file named QuizScores.vb using Notepad or the text editor of your choice.

2. Write the bubble sort.

3. Output the student's name and eight highest quiz scores.

4. Save this source code file in a directory of your choice, and then make that directory your working directory.

5. Compile the source code file, QuizScores.vb.

6. Execute the program with the following input, and record the output.

   Student Name: Dan Williams

   Ten Quiz Scores: 75, 32, 78, 92, 80, 77, 92, 92, 86, 99

Using Multidimensional Arrays

As you learned in Chapter 8 of *Programming Logic and Design, Sixth Edition*, an array whose elements are accessed using a single subscript is called a **one-dimensional array** or a **single-dimensional array**. You also learned that a **two-dimensional array** stores elements in two dimensions and requires two subscripts to access elements.

In Chapter 8 of *Programming Logic and Design, Sixth Edition*, you saw how useful two-dimensional arrays can be when you studied the example of owning an apartment building with five floors with each floor having studio, one-bedroom, and two-bedroom apartments. The rent charged for these apartments depends on which floor the apartment is located as well as the number of bedrooms the apartment has. Table 8-1 shows the rental amounts.

Floor	Studio Apartment	1-Bedroom Apartment	2-Bedroom Apartment
0	350	390	435
1	400	440	480
2	475	530	575
3	600	650	700
4	1000	1075	1150

Table 8-1   Rent schedule based on floor and number of bedrooms

In Visual Basic, declaring a two-dimensional array to store the rents shown in Table 8-1 requires two integer values within parentheses and separated by a comma. The first integer value represents the number of rows in the array, and the second integer value represents the number of columns. The declaration is shown below.

```
Dim FLOORS As Integer = 5
Dim BEDROOMS As Integer = 3
Dim rent(FLOORS,BEDROOMS) As Double
```

The declaration shows the array's name, rent, followed by a pair of parentheses. Within the parentheses, the number of rows is represented by the first integer (FLOORS) followed by a comma; the number of columns is represented by the second integer (BEDROOMS).

As shown below, you can also initialize a two-dimensional array when you declare it by enclosing a comma within the parentheses that follow the name of the array and then enclosing all of the values within a pair of curly braces and also enclosing the values (separated by commas) for each row within curly braces. Notice that each group of values within curly braces is separated by commas.

```
Dim rent(,) As Double = {{350, 390, 435},
                          {400, 440, 480},
                          {475, 530, 575},
                          {600, 650, 700},
                          {1000, 1075, 1150}}
```

To access individual elements in the rent array, two subscripts are required as shown below.

```
Dim myRent As Double
myRent = rent(3,1)
```

Remember that in Visual Basic, array subscripts begin with 0.

The first subscript (3) determines the row, and the second subscript (1) determines the column. In the assignment statement, myRent = rent(3,1), the value 650 is assigned to the variable named myRent.

Figure 8-3 shows the pseudocode for a program that continuously displays rents for apartments based on renter requests for bedrooms and floor. Figure 8-4 shows the Visual Basic code that implements the program.

```
start
   Declarations
      num RENT_BY_FLOOR_AND_BDRMS[5][3] = {350, 390, 435},
                                           {400, 440, 480},
                                           {475, 530, 575},
                                           {600, 650, 700},
                                           {1000, 1075, 1150}
      num floor
      num bedrooms
      num QUIT = 99
   getReady()
   while floor <> QUIT
      determineRent()
   endwhile
   finish()
stop

getReady()
   output "Enter floor "
   input floor
return

determineRent()
   output "Enter number of bedrooms "
   input bedrooms
```

Figure 8-3   Pseudocode for a program that determines rents (continues)

(continued)

```
    output "Rent is $", RENT_BY_FLOOR_AND_BDRMS[floor][bedrooms]
    output "Enter floor "
    input floor
return

finish()
    output "End of program"
return
```

Figure 8-3 Pseudocode for a program that determines rents

```
Option Explicit On
Option Strict On
Module DetermineRent
    Sub Main()
        ' Declare variables.
        Dim rent(,) As Double ={{350, 390, 435}, _
                                {400, 440, 480}, _
                                {475, 530, 575}, _
                                {600, 650, 700}, _
                                {1000, 1075, 1150}}
        Dim floor As Integer
        Dim bedroom As Integer
        Dim floorString As String
        Dim bedroomString As String
        Dim QUIT As Integer = 99

        ' Work done in the getReady() procedure
        floorString = InputBox$("Enter floor or 99 to quit: ")
        floor = Convert.ToInt32(floorString)

        Do While floor <> QUIT
            ' Work done in the determineRent() procedure
            bedroomString = InputBox$( _
                            "Enter number of bedrooms: ")
            bedroom = Convert.ToInt32(bedroomString)
            System.Console.WriteLine("Rent is $" & _
                            rent(floor,bedroom))
            floorString = InputBox$( _
                            "Enter floor or 99 to quit: ")
            floor = Convert.ToInt32(floorString)
        Loop
        ' Work done in the finish() procedure
        System.Console.WriteLine("End of program")
    End Sub ' End of Main() procedure.
End Module ' End of DetermineRent module.
```

Figure 8-4 Visual Basic code for a program that determines rents

Exercise 8-3: Using Multidimensional Arrays

In this exercise, you use what you have learned about using multi-dimensional arrays to answer Questions 1–3.

1. A two-dimensional array declared as
   `Dim myNums(3,2) As Integer` has how many rows?

   _____

2. A two-dimensional array declared as
   `Dim myNums(3,2) As Integer` has how many columns?

   _____

3. Consider the following array declaration,
   `Dim myNums(3,2) As Integer`

   Are the following Visual Basic statements legal?

   ```
   number = myNums(3,2)    _____
   number = myNums(0,1)    _____
   number = myNums(1,2)    _____
   ```

LAB 8.3   Using Multidimensional Arrays

In this lab, you will complete a Visual Basic program that uses a two-dimensional array to store data for the MidAmerica Bus Company. The program is described in Chapter 8, Exercise 8 in *Programming Logic and Design, Sixth Edition*. The bus company charges fares to passengers based on the number of travel zones they cross. Additionally, it provides discounts for multiple passengers traveling together. The ticket prices are shown in Table 8-2.

Passengers	Zones Crossed			
	0	1	2	3
1	7.50	10.00	12.00	12.75
2	14.00	18.50	22.00	23.00
3	20.00	21.00	32.00	33.00
4	25.00	27.50	36.00	37.00

Table 8-2   Ticket prices for Lab 8.3

The program should allow users to enter the number of passengers and the number of travel zones they will cross on their trip. The program should output the ticket charge. The file provided for this lab contains all of the necessary variable declarations, except the two-dimensional array, and it also includes a priming read input statement. You need to write the code that initializes the two-dimensional array, retrieves additional input from the user, determines the ticket charge, and prints the ticket charge. Comments in the code tell you where to write your statements.

1. Open the source code file named Tickets.vb using Notepad or the text editor of your choice.

2. Declare and initialize the two-dimensional array.

3. Write the Visual Basic statements that retrieve the number of passengers and the number of travel zones crossed.

4. Determine and print the ticket charge.

5. Save this source code file in a directory of your choice, and then make that directory your working directory.

6. Compile the source code file Tickets.vb.

7. Execute the program.

CHAPTER 9

Advanced Modularization Techniques

After studying this chapter, you will be able to:

◎ Write procedures that require no parameters

◎ Write procedures that require a single parameter

◎ Write procedures that require multiple parameters

◎ Write functions that return values

◎ Pass entire arrays and single elements of an array to a procedure or function

◎ Use Visual Basic's built-in functions

In Chapter 2 of *Programming Logic and Design, Sixth Edition*, you learned that local variables are variables that are declared within the procedure that uses them. You also learned that most programs consist of a main procedure, which contains the mainline logic and calls other subroutines to get specific work done in the program.

In this chapter, you learn more about procedures. You also learn about functions and how they differ from procedures. You learn how to write procedures and functions that require no parameters, how to write procedures that require a single parameter, how to write procedures and functions that require multiple parameters, and how to write functions that return a value. You also learn how to pass an array to a procedure or function and how to use some of Visual Basic's built-in functions. To help you learn about procedures and functions, you will study some Visual Basic programs that implement the logic and design presented in *Programming Logic and Design, Sixth Edition*.

You should do the exercises and labs in this chapter after you have finished Chapter 9 of *Programming Logic and Design, Sixth Edition*.

Writing Procedures with No Parameters

A procedure is a block of Visual Basic code that performs some task but does not return a value. (In other languages, procedures are often called subroutines.) Code that is repeated more than once in a program belongs in a procedure. Similarly, when you have some code that you could use in more than one program, you should put it into a procedure. Using procedures in this way makes it easier for you and other programmers to read and maintain your code.

To review what you already learned about procedures, let us examine the Visual Basic code for the Customer Bill program shown in Figure 9-1. Notice the line numbers in front of each line of code in this program. These line numbers are not actually part of the program but are included for reference only.

```
1 Module CustomerBill
2    Sub Main()
3       ' Declare variables local to Main()
4       Dim name As String
5       Dim balanceString As String
6       Dim balance As Double
7
8       ' Get interactive input
9       name = InputBox$("Enter customer's name: ")
```

Figure 9-1   Visual Basic code for the Customer Bill program *(continues)*

146

(continued)

```
10          balanceString = InputBox$( _
11                        "Enter customer's balance: ")
12          ' Convert String to Double
13          balance = Convert.ToDouble(balanceString)
14
15          ' Call nameAndAddress() procedure
16          nameAndAddress()
17
18          ' Output customer name and address
19          System.Console.WriteLine("Customer Name:  " & name)
20          System.Console.WriteLine("Customer Balance:  " & _
21                                    balance)
22      End Sub   ' End of Main() procedure
23
24      Sub nameAndAddress()
25          ' Declare and initialize local, constant Strings
26          Const ADDRESS_LINE1 As String = "ABC Manufacturing"
27          Const ADDRESS_LINE2 As String = "47 Industrial Lane"
28          Const ADDRESS_LINE3 As String = "Wild Rose, WI 54984"
29
30          ' Output
31          System.Console.WriteLine(ADDRESS_LINE1)
32          System.Console.WriteLine(ADDRESS_LINE2)
33          System.Console.WriteLine(ADDRESS_LINE3)
34      End Sub   ' End of nameAndAddress() procedure
35 End Module
```

Figure 9-1   Visual Basic code for the Customer Bill program

The program begins execution with the Main() procedure, which is shown on line 2. This procedure contains the declaration of three variables (lines 4, 5, and 6), name, balanceString, and balance, which are local to the Main() procedure. Next, on lines 9, 10, and 11, interactive input statements retrieve values for name and balanceString, and, on line 13, balanceString is converted to the Double data type and assigned to the variable named balance. The procedure nameAndAddress() is then called on line 16, with no arguments listed within its parentheses. Remember that arguments, which are sometimes called **actual parameters**, are data items sent to procedures. There are no arguments for the nameAndAddress() procedure because this procedure requires no data. You learn about passing arguments to procedures later in this chapter. The last two statements (lines 19, 20, and 21) in the Main() procedure are print statements that output the customer's name and balance.

Next, on line 24, you see the header for the nameAndAddress() procedure. The **header** begins with the Sub keyword followed by the procedure name, which is nameAndAddress(). The nameAndAddress() procedure does not return a value. You learn about functions that return values later in this chapter.

Also, notice that there are no formal parameters within the parentheses. Remember that **formal parameters** are the variables in the procedure header that accept the values from the actual parameters. (You learn about writing procedures that accept parameters in the next section of this chapter.) In the next part of the Customer Bill program, we see three constants that are local to the nameAndAddress() procedure: ADDRESS_LINE1, ADDRESS_LINE2, and ADDRESS_LINE3. These constants are declared and initialized on lines 26, 27, and 28, and then printed on lines 31, 32, and 33. When the input to this program is Ed Gonzales (name) and 352.39 (balance), the output is as shown in Figure 9-2.

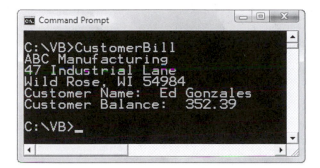

Figure 9-2   Output from the Customer Bill program

Exercise 9-1: Writing Procedures with No Parameters

In this exercise, you use what you have learned about writing procedures with no parameters to answer Questions 1–2.

1. Given the following procedure calls, write the procedure's header:

    a. printBusinessCard()

    _____

    b. displayCustomerInfo()

    _____

    c. displayRecipe()

    _____

2. Given the following procedure headers, write a procedure call:

    a. Sub displayStudentAddress()

    _____

b.   Sub printRoster()

_____

c.   Sub displayEmployeeNames()

_____

LAB 9.1 Writing Procedures with No Parameters

In this lab, you complete a partially prewritten Visual Basic program that includes simple procedures. The program prompts the user for his or her age. If the user is 18 or older, the program should call a procedure named canVote() that displays the message "You are old enough to vote in this election." If the user is younger than 18, the program should call a procedure named cannotVote() that displays the message "Sorry, you'll have to wait to vote until you are 18." The source code file provided for this lab includes the necessary variable declarations and the input statement. Comments are included in the file to help you write the remainder of the program.

1. Open the source code file named AllowVote.vb using Notepad or the text editor of your choice.

2. Write the Visual Basic statements as indicated by the comments.

3. Save this source code file in a directory of your choice, and then make that directory your working directory.

4. Compile the source code file AllowVote.vb.

5. Execute the program.

Writing Procedures that Require a Single Parameter

As you learned in *Programming Logic and Design, Sixth Edition*, some procedures require data to accomplish their task. You also learned that designing a program so that it sends data (which can be different each time the program runs) to a procedure (which doesn't change) keeps you from having to write multiple procedures to handle similar situations. For example, suppose you are writing a program that has to determine if a number is even or odd. It is certainly better to write a single procedure, to which the program can pass a number entered by the user, than to write individual procedures for every number.

In Figure 9-3, you see the Visual Basic code for a program that includes a procedure that can determine if a number is odd or even. The line numbers are not actually part of the program but are included for reference only. The program allows the user to enter a number, and then passes that number to a procedure as an argument. After it receives the argument, the procedure can determine if the number is an even number or an odd number.

```
1 Module EvenOrOdd
2    Sub Main()
3        Dim   number As Integer
4        Dim numberString As String
5
6        numberString = InputBox$( _
7                       "Enter a number or -999 to quit: ")
8        number = Convert.ToInt32(numberString)
9
10       Do While number <> -999
11           EvenOrOdd(number)
12           numberString = InputBox$( _
13                          "Enter a number or -999 to quit: ")
14           number = Convert.ToInt32(numberString)
15       Loop
16   End Sub   ' End of Main() subroutine.
17
18   Sub EvenOrOdd(ByVal number As Integer)
19       If number Mod 2 = 0
20           System.Console.WriteLine("Number: " & number & _
21                                    " is even.")
22       Else
23           System.Console.WriteLine("Number: " & number & _
24                                    " is odd.")
25       End If
26   End Sub   ' End of EvenOrOdd subroutine
27 End Module  ' End of EvenOrOdd module
```

> The variable named **number** is local to the Main() procedure. Its value is stored at one memory location. For example, it may be stored at memory location 2000.

> The value of the formal parameter, **number**, is stored at a different memory location and is local to the EvenOrOdd() method. For example, it may be stored at memory location 7800.

Figure 9-3   Visual Basic code for the Even Or Odd program

On lines 6 and 7 in this program, the user is asked to enter a number or, when he or she is finished entering numbers and wants to quit the program, the sentinel value, −999. (You learned about sentinel values in Chapter 5 of this book.) On lines 6, 7, and 8, the input value is retrieved, stored in the variable named numberString, converted to an Integer, and then stored in the variable named number. Next, if the user did not enter the sentinel value −999, the Do While loop is entered, and the procedure named EvenOrOdd() is called (line 11) using the following syntax: EvenOrOdd(number).

Notice that the variable number is placed within the parentheses, which means that number is passed to the EvenOrOdd() procedure. Within the procedure, the value is stored in the formal parameter at a different memory location, and is considered local to that procedure. In this example, as shown on line 18, the value is stored in the formal parameter named number.

The data type of the formal parameter and the actual parameter must be the same.

Program control is now transferred to the EvenOrOdd() procedure. The header for the EvenOrOdd() procedure on line 18 includes the Sub keyword, as discussed earlier in this chapter. The name of the procedure follows. Within the parentheses that follow the procedure name, the keyword ByVal is followed by the parameter number, which is given a local name and declared as the Integer data type.

Remember that even though the name of the parameter number has the same name as the local variable number in the Main() procedure, they are stored at different memory locations. Figure 9-3 shows that the variable number that is local to Main() is stored at one memory location, and the parameter number in the EvenOrOdd() procedure is stored at a different memory location. The keyword ByVal indicates that the argument is passed by value to this procedure. **Passing an argument by value** means that a copy of the value of the argument is passed to the procedure.

Within the procedure on line 19, the modulus operator Mod is used in the test portion of the If statement to determine if the value of the local number is even or odd. You learned about the Mod operator in Chapter 2 of this book. The user is then informed if number is even (lines 20 and 21) or odd (lines 23 and 24), and program control is transferred back to the statement that follows the call to EvenOrOdd() in the Main() procedure (line 12).

Back in the Main() procedure, the user is asked to enter another number on lines 12 and 13, and the Do While loop continues to execute, calling the EvenOrOdd() procedure with a new input value. The loop is exited when the user enters the sentinel value −999, and the program ends. When the input to this program is 45, 98, 1, −32, 643, and −999, the output is as shown in Figure 9-4.

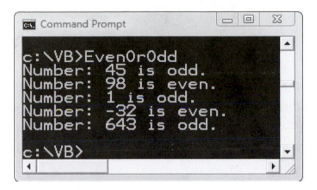

Figure 9-4 Output from the Even Or Odd program

Exercise 9-2: Writing Procedures that Require a Single Parameter

In this exercise, you use what you have learned about writing procedures that require a single parameter to answer Questions 1–2.

1. Given the following variable declarations and procedure calls, write the procedure's header:

    a. `Dim name As String`

        `printNameBadge(name)`

        _____

    b. `Dim side_length As Double`

        `calculateRectangleArea(side_length)`

        _____

    c. `Dim hours As Integer`

        `displaySecondsInHours(hours)`

        _____

2. Given the following procedure headers, write a procedure call:

    a. `Sub displayPetName(ByVal petName As String)`

        _____

    b. `Sub printHolidays(ByVal year As Integer)`

        _____

    c. `Sub checkValidPassword(ByVal password As String)`

        _____

LAB 9.2 Writing Procedures that Require a Single Parameter

In this lab, you complete a partially written Visual Basic program that includes a procedure requiring a single parameter. The program prompts the user for an integer. If the integer is divisible by 9, the program calls a procedure named divide(). This procedure displays the message "number divided by 9 is result", where number is the value of number and result is the value of result. If number is not divisible by 9, the message "Sorry, number is not divisible by 9" is displayed, where number is the value of number. The source code file provided for this lab includes the necessary variable declarations and the input statement. Comments are included in the file to help you write the remainder of the program.

1. Open the source code file named DivideByNine.vb using Notepad or the text editor of your choice.

2. Write the Visual Basic statements as indicated by the comments.

3. Save this source code file in a directory of your choice, and then make that directory your working directory.

4. Compile the source code file DivideByNine.vb.

5. Execute the program.

Writing Procedures that Require Multiple Parameters

In Chapter 9 of *Programming Logic and Design, Sixth Edition*, you learned that a procedure often requires more than one parameter in order to accomplish its task. To specify that a procedure requires multiple parameters, you include a list of data types and local identifiers separated by commas as part of the procedure's header. To call a procedure that expects multiple parameters, you list the actual parameters (separated by commas) in the call to the procedure.

In Figure 9-5, you see the Visual Basic code for a program that includes a procedure named computeTax() that you designed in *Programming Logic and Design, Sixth Edition*. The line numbers are not actually part of the program but are included for reference only.

```
 1 Module ComputeTax
 2    Sub Main()
 3       Dim balance As Double ─────────────────────── Memory address 1000
 4       Dim balanceString As String
 5       Dim rate As Double ──────────────────────────── Memory address 1008
 6       Dim rateString As String
 7
 8       balanceString = InputBox$("Enter balance: ")
 9       balance = Convert.ToDouble(balanceString)
10       rateString = InputBox$("Enter rate: ")
11       rate = Convert.ToDouble(rateString)
12
13       computeTax(balance, rate)
14
15    End Sub ' End of Main() procedure.
16                                                        Memory address 9000
17    Sub computeTax(ByVal amount As Double, _
18                   ByVal rate As Double)
19       Dim tax As Double
20                                                        Memory address 9008
21       tax = amount * rate
22       System.Console.WriteLine("Amount: " & amount & _
23                             " Rate: " & rate & _
24                             " Tax: " & tax)
25    End Sub    ' End of computeTax procedure
26 End Module    ' End of ComputeTax module
```

Figure 9-5   Visual Basic code for the Compute Tax program

In the Visual Basic code shown in Figure 9-5, you see that the
highlighted call to computeTax() on line 13 includes the names
of the local variables balance and rate within the parentheses
and that they are separated by a comma. These are the arguments
(actual parameters) that are passed to the computeTax() procedure. You can also see that the computeTax() procedure header on
lines 17 and 18 is highlighted and includes two formal parameters,
ByVal amount As Double and ByVal rate As Double, listed within
parentheses and separated by a comma. The value of the variable
named balance is passed by value to the computeTax() procedure
as an actual parameter and is stored in the formal parameter named
amount. The value of the variable named rate is passed by value to
the computeTax() procedure as an actual parameter and is stored
in the formal parameter named rate. As illustrated in Figure 9-5, it
does not matter that one of the parameters being passed, rate, has
the same name as the parameter received, rate, because they occupy
different memory locations. When the input to this program is 300.00
(balance) and .12 (rate), the output is shown in Figure 9-6.

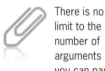

In Visual Basic, when you write a procedure that expects more than one parameter, you must list a data type for each parameter, even if the data types for each parameter are the same.

154

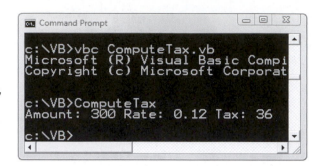

Figure 9-6 Output from the Compute Tax program

Exercise 9-3: Writing Procedures that Require Multiple Parameters

In this exercise, you use what you have learned about writing procedures that require multiple parameters to answer Questions 1–2.

There is no limit to the number of arguments you can pass to a procedure, but when multiple arguments are passed to a procedure, the call to the procedure and the procedure's header must match. This means that the number of arguments, their data types, and the order in which they are listed must all be the same.

1. Given the following procedure calls, write the procedure's header:

   a. `Dim name As String`

       `Dim title As String`

       `printNameBadge(name, title)`

       _____

   b. `Dim one_length As Double`

       `Dim two_length As Double`

       `calculateSquareArea(one_length, two_length)`

       _____

   c. `Dim day As Integer`

       `Dim month As Integer`

       `Dim year As Integer`

       `Dim amount As Double`

       `printBill(day, month, year, amount)`

       _____

2. Given the following procedure headers, write a procedure call:

    a. `Sub studentInfo(ByVal name As String, _`
        `ByVal tuition As Double)`

        _____

    b. `Sub printProduct(ByVal num1 As Integer, _`
        `ByVal num2 As Integer)`

        _____

    c. `Sub decrease(ByVal bal As Double, _`
        `ByVal payment As Double)`

        _____

LAB 9.3 Writing Procedures that Require Multiple Parameters

In this lab, you complete a partially written Visual Basic program that includes a procedure requiring multiple parameters (arguments). The program prompts the user for an item price and the number of items ordered. If the item's price is less than $5.00, the program should apply a 4% discount; if the item's price is between $5.00 and $9.99, the program should apply a 7% discount; if the item is $10.00 or more, the program should apply a 10% discount. Once the discount is applied, the program should calculate the total price for the number of items purchased and then display the original price, the discount percent, the discounted price, the quantity ordered, and the total price for the items ordered. The source code file provided for this lab includes the variable declarations and the input statements. Comments are included in the file to help you write the remainder of the program.

1. Open the source code file named `DiscountPrices.vb` using Notepad or the text editor of your choice.

2. Write the Visual Basic statements as indicated by the comments.

3. Save this source code file in a directory of your choice, and then make that directory your working directory.

4. Compile the source code file `DiscountPrices.vb`.

5. Execute the program.

Writing Functions that Return a Value

Thus far, this chapter has focused on taking blocks of code that you might need to use repeatedly and writing them as procedures. As you have learned, Visual Basic procedures cannot return a value. When your program requires you to repeatedly use a block of code that *does* return a value, you can write the code as a function instead.

A **function** is a block of code that performs some task and returns a value. A function can only return a single value; when you write the code for the function, you must indicate the data type of the value you want to return. This is often referred to as the function's return type. The return type can be any of Visual Basic's built-in data types, as well as a class type. You learn more about classes in Chapter 10 of this book. For now, we focus on returning values of the built-in types.

In Chapter 9 of *Programming Logic and Design, Sixth Edition*, you studied the design for a program that includes a method named getHoursWorked(). This method is designed to prompt a user for the number of hours an employee has worked, retrieve the value, and then return that value to the location in the program where the method was called. The Visual Basic code that implements this design is shown in Figure 9-7.

```
1 Module GrossPay
2    Sub Main()
3       Dim hours As Double
4       Const PAY_RATE As Double = 12.00
5       Dim gross As Double
6
7       hours = getHoursWorked()
8       gross = hours * PAY_RATE
9
10      System.Console.WriteLine("Hours worked: " & hours)
11      System.Console.WriteLine("Gross pay is: " & gross)
12   End Sub ' End of Main() procedure
13
14   Function getHoursWorked() As Double
15      Dim workHoursString As String
16
17      workHoursString = InputBox$( _
18                        "Please enter hours worked: ")
19      Return Convert.ToDouble(workHoursString)
20   End Function  ' End of getHoursWorked function
21 End Module   ' End of GrossPay module
```

Figure 9-7 Visual Basic code for a program that includes the getHoursWorked() function

The Visual Basic program shown in Figure 9-7 declares local variables `hours`, `PAY_RATE`, and `gross` on lines 3, 4, and 5 in the `Main()` procedure. The next statement (line 7), shown below, is an assignment statement:

```
hours = getHoursWorked()
```

This assignment statement includes a call to the function named `getHoursWorked()`. As with all assignment statements, the expression on the right side of the assignment operator (`=`) is evaluated, and then the result is assigned to the variable named on the left side of the assignment operator (`=`). In this example, the expression on the right is a call to the `getHoursWorked()` function.

When the `getHoursWorked()` function is called, program control is transferred to the function. Notice that the header (line 14) for this function is written as follows:

```
Function getHoursWorked() As Double
```

The keyword `Function` is used in the header to specify that what follows is a function. The name of the function comes next, followed by parentheses. The `getHoursWorked()` function has no parameters within the parentheses because nothing is passed to this function. The keyword `As` follows the parentheses, and then the data type that this function returns. In this example, a value of data type `Double` is returned by the `getHoursWorked()` function.

A local variable, `workHoursString`, is then declared on line 15. On lines 17 and 18, the user is asked to enter the number of hours worked, at which point the value is retrieved and stored in `workHoursString`. Next, on line 19, you see the `Return` statement followed by the `Convert.ToDouble()` method that is responsible for converting `workHoursString` to a `Double`. The `Return` statement causes this `Double` value to be returned to the location in the calling procedure where `getHoursWorked()` is called, which is the right side of the assignment statement on line 7.

The value returned to the right side of the assignment statement is then assigned to the variable named `hours` (data type `Double`) in the `Main()` procedure. Next, the gross pay is calculated on line 8, followed by the `System.Console.WriteLine()` statements on lines 10 and 11 that display the value of the local variables `hours` and `gross`, which contain the number of hours worked and the calculated gross pay.

You can also use a function's return value directly rather than store it in a variable. The two Visual Basic statements that follow make calls to the same `getHoursWorked()` function shown in Figure 9-7, but in these statements the returned value is used directly in the statement that calculates gross pay and in the statement that prints the returned value.

```
gross = getHoursWorked() * PAY_RATE
System.Console.WriteLine("Hours worked is " & _
getHoursWorked())
```

When the input to this program is 45, the output is shown in Figure 9-8.

Figure 9-8 Output from program that includes the getHoursWorked() function

Exercise 9-4: Writing Functions that Return a Value

In this exercise, you use what you have learned about writing functions that return a value to answer Questions 1–2.

1. Given the following variable declarations and function calls, write the function's header:

    a. `Dim price As Double`

        `Dim percent As Double`

        `Dim newPrice As Double`

        `newPrice = calculatePriceIncrease(price, percent)`

        _____

    b. `Dim area As Double`

        `Dim one_length As Double`

        `Dim two_length As Double`

        `area = figureArea(one_length, two_length)`

        _____

c. `Dim lower_case As String`

   `Dim upper_case As String`

   `upper_case = changeCase(lower_case)`

   _____

2. Given the following function headers, write a function call:

   a. `Function findCustomerType(ByVal custNumber _`
      `As Integer) As String`

      _____

   b. `Function product(ByVal num1 As Integer, _`
      `ByVal num2 As Integer) As Integer`

      _____

   c. `Function power(ByVal num As Integer, _`
      `ByVal exp As Integer) As Integer`

      _____

LAB 9.4 Writing Functions that Return a Value

In this lab, you complete a partially written Visual Basic program that includes a function that returns a value. The program is a simple calculator that prompts the user for two numbers and an operator (+, -, *, /, or \). The two numbers and the operator are passed to the function where the appropriate arithmetic operation is performed. The result is then returned to the `Main()` procedure where the arithmetic operation and result are displayed. For example, if the user enters 3, 4, and *, the following is displayed:

3.00 * 4.00 = 12.00

The source code file provided for this lab includes the necessary variable declarations, and input and output statements. Comments are included in the file to help you write the remainder of the program.

1. Open the source code file named `Arithmetic.vb` using Notepad or the text editor of your choice.

2. Write the Visual Basic statements as indicated by the comments.

3. Save this source code file in a directory of your choice, and then make that directory your working directory.

4. Compile the source code file `Arithmetic.vb`.

5. Execute the program.

Passing an Array and an Array Element to a Procedure or Function

As a Visual Basic programmer, there are times when you will want to write a procedure or function that will perform a task on all of the elements you have stored in an array. For example, in Chapter 9 of *Programming Logic and Design, Sixth Edition*, you saw a design for a program that used a procedure to quadruple all of the values stored in an array. This design is translated into Visual Basic code in Figure 9-9.

```
1 Module PassEntireArray
2    Sub Main()
3       ' Declare variables
4       Const LENGTH As Integer = 4
5       Dim someNums() As Integer = {10, 12, 22, 35}
6       Dim x As Integer
7
8       System.Console.WriteLine( _
9             "At beginning of main procedure. . . ")
10      x = 0
11      ' This loop prints initial array values
12      Do While x < LENGTH
13         System.Console.WriteLine(someNums(x))
14         x = x + 1
15      Loop
16      ' Call procedure, pass array
17      quadrupleTheValues(someNums)
18
19      System.Console.WriteLine( _
20            "At the end of main procedure. . . ")
21      x = 0
22      ' This loop prints changed array values
23      Do While x < somenums.Length
24         System.Console.WriteLine(someNums(x))
25         x = x + 1
26      Loop
27   End Sub   ' End of Main() procedure
28
```

Figure 9-9   Visual Basic code for the Pass Entire Array program (*continues*)

(continued)

```
29      Sub quadrupleTheValues(ByRef vals() As Integer)
30          Const LENGTH As Integer = 4
31          Dim x As Integer
32
33          x = 0
34          ' This loop prints array values before they're changed
35          Do While x < LENGTH
36              System.Console.WriteLine( _
37                      "  In quadrupleTheValues() procedure, " & _
38                      "value is " & vals(x))
39              x = x + 1
40          Loop
41          x = 0
42          Do While x < LENGTH   ' This loop changes array values
43              vals(x) = vals(x) * 4
44              x = x + 1
45          Loop
46          x = 0
47          ' This loop prints array values after they're changed
48          Do While x < LENGTH
49              System.Console.WriteLine( _
50                      "  After change, value is " & vals(x))
51              x = x + 1
52          Loop
53      End Sub    ' End of quadrupleTheValues procedure
54 End Module    ' End of PassEntireArray module
```

Figure 9-9   Visual Basic code for the Pass Entire Array program

The Main() procedure begins on line 2 and proceeds with the declaration and initialization of the constant named LENGTH (line 4) and the array of integers named someNums (line 5), followed by the declaration of the variable named x (line 6), which is used as a loop control variable. The first Do While loop in the program on lines 12 through 15 is responsible for printing the values stored in the array at the beginning of the program. Next, on line 17, the procedure named quadrupleTheValues() is called. The array named someNums is passed as an argument. Notice that when an entire array is passed to a procedure, the parentheses and the size are not included. Also note that when you pass an entire array to a procedure, the array may be passed by value or passed by reference.

In this example, the array is **passed by reference**, which means that instead of a copy of the array being passed, the memory address of the array is passed. This gives the procedure access to that memory location; the procedure can then change the values stored in the array if necessary.

Program control is then transferred to the quadrupleTheValues() procedure. The header for the procedure on line 29 includes one parameter, ByRef vals() As Integer. The syntax for declaring an

You may pass all data types (e.g., Integer, Double, String) by value or by reference.

array as a formal parameter that is passed by reference includes the keyword `ByRef`, followed by a local name for the array, followed by empty parentheses, followed by the keyword `As`, and then the parameter's data type. Note that a size is not included within the parentheses. In the `quadrupleTheValues()` procedure, the first `Do While` loop on lines 35 through 40 prints the values stored in the array, and the second `Do While` loop on lines 42 through 45 accesses each element in the array, quadruples the value, and then stores the quadrupled values in the array at their same location. The third `Do While` loop on lines 48 through 52 prints the changed values now stored in the array. Program control is then returned to the location in the `Main()` procedure where the `quadrupleTheValues()` procedure was called.

When program control returns to the `Main()` procedure, the next statements to execute (lines 19 through 26) are responsible for printing out the values stored in the array once more. The output from this program is displayed in Figure 9-10.

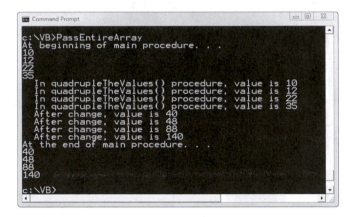

Figure 9-10   Output from the Pass Entire Array program

As shown in Figure 9-10, the array values printed at the beginning of the `Main()` procedure (lines 12 through 15) are the values with which the array was initialized. Next, the `quadrupleTheValues()` procedure prints the array values (lines 35 through 40) again before they are changed. As shown, the values remain the same as the initialized values. The `quadrupleTheValues()` procedure then prints the array values again after the values are quadrupled (lines 48 through 52). Finally, after the call to `quadrupleTheValues()`, the `Main()` procedure prints the array values one last time (lines 23 through 26). These are the quadrupled values, indicating that the `quadrupleTheValues()` procedure has access to the memory location where the array is stored and is able to permanently change the values stored there.

You can also pass a single array element to a procedure or function, just as you pass a variable or constant. The following Visual Basic code initializes an array named someNums, declares a variable named newNum, and passes one element of the array to a function named tripleTheNumber():

```
Dim someNums()As Integer = {10, 12, 22, 35}
Dim newNum As Integer
newNum = tripleTheNumber(someNums(1))
```

The following Visual Basic code includes the header for the function named tripleTheNumber() along with the code that triples the value passed to it:

```
Function tripleTheNumber(ByVal num As Integer) As Integer
    Return num * 3
End Function
```

Exercise 9-5: Passing Arrays to Procedures and Functions

In this exercise, you use what you have learned about passing arrays and array elements to procedures and functions to answer Questions 1–3.

1. Given the following procedure or function calls, write the procedure or function header:

    a. `Dim septemberDueDates () As Integer = {3, 12, 13, _`
        `22, 27, 31}`

        `printDueDates(septemberDueDates)`

        _____

    b. `Dim febInvoices () As Double = {100.00, 200.00, _`
        `55.00, 230.00}`

        `total = monthlyIncome(febInvoices)`

        _____

    c. `Dim overdue() As Double = {34.56, 33.22, 65.77, _`
        `89.99}`

        `printNotice(overdue[1])`

        _____

2. Given the following procedure or function headers, write a procedure or function call:

    a. ```
        Sub Student(ByVal name() As String, _
        ByVal grades() As Double)
        ```

    _____

    b.  ```
        Function printAverage(ByVal nums() As Integer) _
        As Integer
        ```

    _____

3. Given the following procedure header (in which sal is one element of an array of Doubles), write a procedure call:

    a. ```
        Sub increase(ByVal sal As Double)
        ```

    _____

## LAB 9.5  Passing Arrays to Procedures and Functions

In this lab, you complete a partially written Visual Basic program that prints student grade reports. The program passes two parallel arrays to a procedure where grade reports are printed. One array contains Doubles that represent a student's numeric grade average; the second array contains the names of students, stored as Strings. The procedure prints the student's name followed by his or her letter grade, as shown below:

Name: Maria Frederick – Grade: A

In this program, a student earns letter grades as shown in Table 9-1.

| Numeric Grade | Letter Grade |
|---|---|
| 90–100 | A |
| 80–89 | B |
| 70–79 | C |
| 60–69 | D |
| Less than 60 | F |

**Table 9-1**    Numeric and letter grades

The source code file provided for this lab includes the necessary variable declarations. Comments are included in the file to help you write the remainder of the program.
        ```

1. Open the source code file named `StudentGrades.vb` using Notepad or the text editor of your choice.

2. Write the Visual Basic statements as indicated by the comments.

3. Save this source code file in a directory of your choice, and then make that directory your working directory.

4. Compile the source code file `StudentGrades.vb`.

5. Execute the program.

Using Visual Basic's Built-In Functions

Throughout this book, you have used some of Visual Basic's built-in functions, such as the `WriteLine()` function and the `InputBox$()` function. In this section, we look at another built-in function named `Format()`, which allows you to control the number of places displayed after a decimal point when you print a value of data type `Double`. Using the `Format()` function is just one of several ways within Visual Basic to control the number of places displayed after a decimal point.

In the Test Format program that follows, you see that the `Format()` function expects two arguments: a value to format and a `String` constant. Notice the value to format is a variable named `valToFormat` that is declared as data type `Double`. The string constant used is "`general number`", which is a predefined format that describes how the value should be formatted. The `general number` format displays the `valToFormat` as is, with no thousands separator.

```
Module TestFormat
    Sub Main()
        Dim valToFormat As Double = 1234.3776
        System.Console.WriteLine("General Number: " & _
                Format(valToFormat, "general number"))
        System.Console.WriteLine("Currency: " & _
                Format(valToFormat, "currency"))
        System.Console.WriteLine("Standard: " & _
                Format(valToFormat, "standard"))
        System.Console.WriteLine("Fixed: " & _
                Format(valToFormat, "fixed"))
        System.Console.WriteLine("Percent: " & _
                Format(valToFormat, "percent"))
        System.Console.WriteLine("Scientific: " & _
                Format(valToFormat, "scientific"))
    End Sub ' End of Main() procedure.
End Module ' End of TestFormat module.
```

Table 9-2 lists the Visual Basic predefined formats along with a description of how they format a number.

Format Name	Description
General Number	Displays the number as is, with no thousands separator (,)
Currency	Displays the number with thousands separator (,), if appropriate; displays negative numbers enclosed in parentheses; displays two digits to the right of the decimal point; displays a dollar sign ($) to left of number
Fixed	Displays the number with at least one digit to the left and two digits to the right of the decimal point
Standard	Displays the number with thousands separator (,), if appropriate; displays two digits to the right of the decimal point
Percent	Displays the number multiplied by 100 with a percent sign (%) appended to the right; displays two digits to the right of the decimal point
Scientific	Displays the number using standard scientific notation

Table 9-2 Visual Basic predefined formats

The output of the Test Format program is shown in Figure 9-11. The program can be found in the file named TestFormat.vb.

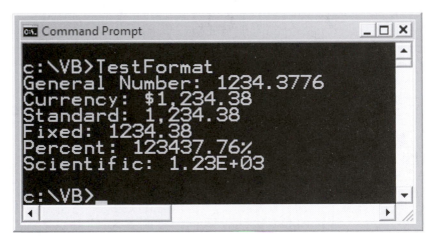

Figure 9-11 Output from the Test Format program

As you continue to learn more about Visual Basic, you will be introduced to many more built-in functions that you can use in your programs.

Exercise 9-6: Using Visual Basic's Built-In Functions

In this exercise, you use a search engine, such as Google, to answer Questions 1–4. Search for some information about a built-in Visual Basic function named StrReverse(). Read the information about the built-in function, and then answer the following questions:

1. What does the StrReverse() function do?

    _____

2. What data type does the StrReverse() function return?

    _____

3. How many arguments does the StrReverse() function require?

    _____

4. What is the data type of the argument(s)?

    _____

LAB 9.6 Using Visual Basic's Built-In Functions

In this lab, you complete a partially written Visual Basic program that includes built-in functions that convert Strings to all uppercase or all lowercase. The program prompts the user to enter any String. To end the program, the user can enter "quit". For each String entered, call the built-in functions LCase() and UCase(). The program should pass a String variable or constant when it calls these functions. Both of these functions return a String with the String changed to uppercase or lowercase. Here is an example:

```
Dim sample As String = "This is a String."
Dim result As String
result = LCase(sample)
result = UCase(sample)
```

The source code file provided for this lab includes the necessary variable declarations and the necessary input and output statements. Comments are included in the file to help you write the remainder of the program.

1. Open the source code file named `UpperAndLower.vb` using Notepad or the text editor of your choice.

2. Write the Visual Basic statements as indicated by the comments.

3. Save this source code file in a directory of your choice, and then make that directory your working directory.

4. Compile the source code file `UpperAndLower.vb`.

5. Execute the program.

Creating a Graphical User Interface (GUI) Using the Visual Studio Integrated Development Environment (IDE)

After studying this chapter, you will be able to:

- ◎ Identify the elements of a Graphical User Interface

- ◎ Identify the major features of the Visual Studio Integrated Development Environment

- ◎ Start Visual Basic, run a Graphical User Interface program, and exit the program

- ◎ Create a simple Graphical User Interface program

- ◎ Create a simple programmer-defined class

A **Graphical User Interface (GUI)** allows users to interact with programs by using a mouse to point, drag, or click. To create a GUI Visual Basic program, you must learn to use Microsoft Visual Studio, which is a programming environment made up of several languages, including Visual Basic, C++, C#, and J#. In this chapter, you examine this environment. You also study the components of a GUI Visual Basic program, run a program, and exit a program. In the process, you will create a simple GUI Visual Basic program and a simple programmer-defined class.

Graphical User Interface Programs

You should do the exercises and labs in this section after you have finished Chapter 12 in *Programming Logic and Design, Sixth Edition*, which discusses creating a GUI. To review briefly, GUI programs are referred to as **event-driven** or **event-based** because they respond to user-initiated events, such as a mouse click. Within a GUI program, an **event listener** waits for an event to occur and then responds to it. An event listener is actually a procedure that contains Visual Basic code that executes when a particular event occurs. For example, when a user of a GUI program clicks a button, an event occurs. In response to the event, the event listener (a procedure that is written as part of the GUI program) executes.

In order to create full-blown event-driven programs that make use of a GUI, you need to learn more about Visual Basic than is included in this book. In this section, you learn to use just a few of the many GUI controls that are included in Visual Basic, such as a button, a textbox, a label, and a form. You also learn to write event listeners that respond to specific user actions, such as clicking.

The Visual Studio Integrated Development Environment

Visual Basic is one of the languages in the integrated software development environment called **Microsoft Visual Studio**. This environment is referred to as an **integrated development environment (IDE)** because it includes not only programming languages but also the tools needed to build forms and to test and debug programs. A **form** is a rectangular area of a screen that serves as a user interface to a program. A form usually includes several elements, such as a title bar, a menu bar, and controls. You learn about these elements later in this chapter.

To begin to learn about the Visual Studio IDE:

- Click the **Start** button on the taskbar, click **All Programs**, and then click **Microsoft Visual Studio 2010**. The Visual Studio Start Page window appears as shown in Figure 10-1.

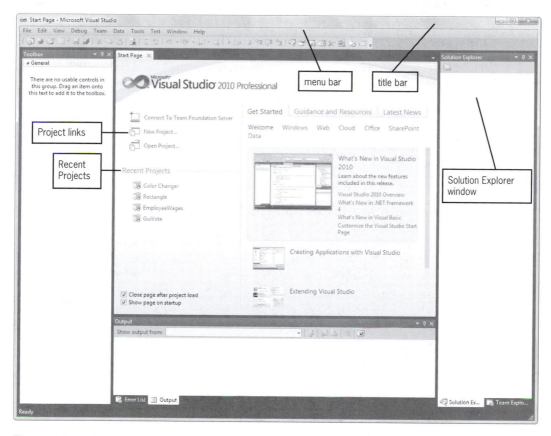

Figure 10-1 The Visual Studio Start Page

As shown in Figure 10-1, the **title bar** at the top of the window contains the name of the window, a system menu, and buttons that you can use to minimize, maximize, or close the window. Below the title bar is the **menu bar**, which includes 10 menus: File, Edit, View, Debug, Team, Data, Tools, Test, Window, and Help. Each menu contains its own list of commands. The menu bar in Visual Studio is **dynamic**, which means the menus and commands change when you work on different tasks.

Beneath the menu bar is the Start Page window. The **Start Page** allows you to open an existing project or create a new one by clicking on one of the projects listed in Recent Projects or clicking on Open Project or New Project. The Start Page is replaced when you open and work on a project. To the right of the Start Page window is the Solution Explorer window. The **Solution Explorer** displays the files that are included in the project you are working on. In Figure 10-1, the Solution Explorer is empty.

Figure 10-1 shows the Visual Studio Start Page window that is displayed using common settings. Your screens may appear different than the ones shown in this textbook.

In addition to menus, you can also use icons on toolbars or shortcut keys to select commands. This book uses menus for most commands.

Components of a Visual Basic Solution

In Chapters 1 through 9, you created Visual Basic programs that were made up of procedures and functions. In the Visual Basic IDE, you work with procedures, projects, and solutions. A **procedure** is a block of Visual Basic code that accomplishes a specific task; a **project** is a collection of procedures; and a **solution** is a collection of projects. The solutions in this book contain only one project, and some of the projects contain only one procedure. For this reason, a project can be thought of as a program, and a procedure can be thought of as a function.

The Solution Folder

To learn about the elements that make up a Visual Basic project, open Microsoft Visual Studio, and then click **Open Project** on the Start Page. This causes the Open Project dialog box to open as shown in Figure 10-2.

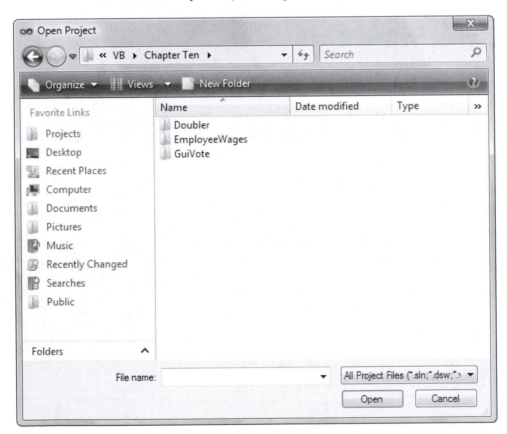

Figure 10-2   A Visual Basic solution folder

In the Open Project dialog box, navigate to the directory where your student files are stored, and find the folder named "GuiVote".

Double-click the **GuiVote** folder to display its contents, double-click the file named **GuiVote.sln,** and then click the **Open** button. The GuiVote solution opens in the Visual Studio Designer window, as shown in Figure 10-3. If a dialog box opens warning you to only open projects from trusted sources, click the **OK** button to continue.

 A file with an .sln file extension is a Visual Basic solution file.

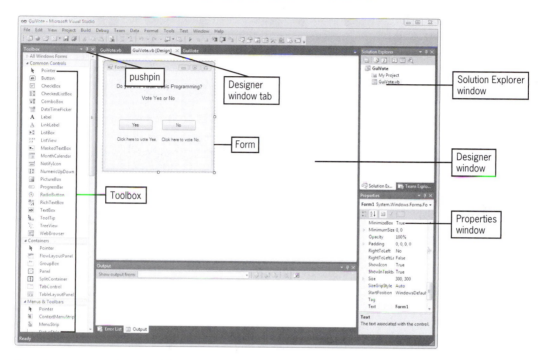

Figure 10-3 Visual Studio Designer window

If you do not see the GuiVote.vb[Design] tab, double-click **GuiVote.vb** in the Solution Explorer window. If your screen does not look like the one shown in Figure 10-3, click the **GuiVote.vb [Design]** tab to switch to the Designer window.

The Designer Window

A Visual Basic programmer uses two windows when working in the Visual Studio IDE. The **Designer window** is used for designing forms, and the **Code window** is used for entering the source code that makes up the program, or solution. We look at the Code window later in this chapter. In Figure 10-3, notice that the form named Form1 is displayed in the Designer window. Notice, too, that GuiVote.vb is highlighted in the Solution Explorer window. The Visual Basic Toolbox is also shown in Figure 10-3, to the left of the Designer window. The Visual Basic **Toolbox** contains the controls you add to a form, such as textboxes, buttons, and labels. A **control** is an object on a form that enables the user to interact with the solution. For example, the "Yes" button is a control.

If you don't see the Toolbox on your screen, click **View** on the menu bar, and then click **Toolbox**. Check the pushpin (also known as Auto Hide) at the top of the Toolbox (shown in Figure 10-3) to be sure that it is pointing down. This causes the Toolbox to remain displayed. If the pushpin is not pointing down, click the pushpin until it does so.

To create Form1, the programmer dragged objects, called controls, from the Toolbox and placed them on the form. There are three label controls and two button controls on Form1. Label controls simply display text. The three label controls on Form1 display the text "Do you like Visual Basic programming? Vote Yes or No.", "Click here to vote Yes.", and "Click here to vote No." Button controls are objects that the user can click. The two button controls on Form1 contain the text "Yes" and "No". If the user of this program clicks the "Yes" button control, the background color of Form1 turns red. If the user clicks the "No" button control, the background color of Form1 turns yellow.

The Code Window

In addition to designing forms, you must also write code in the Code window, so that the controls on the form actually do something when the program executes. To switch from the Designer window to the Code window, click **View** on the menu bar, and then click **Code**. The Code window is shown in Figure 10-4.

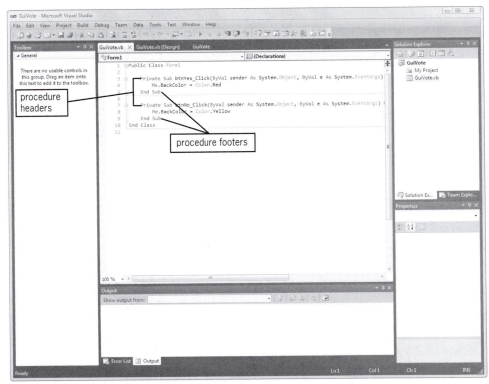

Figure 10-4   Visual Studio Code window

In Figure 10-4, notice the **procedure headers**, which begin with Sub btnYes_Click and Sub btnNo_Click. Also, notice the **procedure footers**, End Sub. The headers mark the beginning of Visual Basic procedures (subroutines) that execute when either the "Yes" or "No" button is clicked on the form. If the user clicks the "Yes" button, the following code executes:

```
Me.BackColor = Color.Red
```

This code causes the background color of the form, Form1, to change to red. If the user clicks the "No" button, the following code executes:

```
Me.BackColor = Color.Yellow
```

This code causes the background color of the form, Form1, to change to yellow.

You can now return to the form in the Designer window by clicking **View** on the menu bar, and then clicking **Designer**.

The Me keyword refers to methods or variables within the current object. In this example, it provides a way to refer to Form1 in which the code is currently executing.

Design-Time and Run-Time Operating Modes

Visual Studio has three modes of operation: design mode, run mode, and break mode. **Design mode** is for creating and modifying a program. **Run mode** is for testing a program by running it. **Break mode** is for debugging large programs, and is beyond the scope of this book.

So far in this chapter, you have been working in design mode. As you have seen, in design mode you can work on a form in the Designer window or you can write code in the Code window.

In run mode, the program is running (executing). In this mode, the form appears as a window on the screen, and you can interact with the program as a user would. Keep in mind that a user never sees a program in the same way a programmer does. When a program is "put into production" (as discussed in *Programming Logic and Design, Sixth Edition*), it is distributed as an executable file, and a user sees nothing but the form (or forms) at run time. You, on the other hand, have two roles: you develop the program by placing controls on a form and writing code that executes in response to a user's action, and you test the program to be sure it executes correctly.

To test the Gui Vote program by executing it, do the following:

1. Click **Debug** on the menu bar, and then click **Start Debugging**. The run-time version of the form is displayed. (You probably also see the **design-time form** of the form

that you have been adding controls to in the background, but do not confuse that with the run-time version.) At this point nothing is happening. That is because the program is waiting for an event to cause a procedure to execute. However, you can tell that you are in run mode because the word "Running" now appears after the name of the program in the Visual Studio title bar.

2. Click the **Yes** button. This causes the btnYes_Click procedure to execute; the background color of the form turns red.

3. Click the **No** button. This causes the btnNo_Click procedure to execute; the background color of the form turns yellow.

4. To stop the program, click **Debug** on the menu bar, then click **Stop Debugging**. The run-time form disappears, and the program returns to design mode.

5. To close the Gui Vote program, click **File** on the menu bar, and then click **Close Project**. Now, you could click the **File** menu where you could create a new project or open an existing project.

6. To close Visual Studio, click **File** on the menu bar, and then click **Exit**.

Creating a Visual Basic IDE Program

In this section, you create a Visual Basic GUI program. This program asks a user to enter a number, which the program then doubles and displays the result.

1. Open Microsoft Visual Studio.

2. On the Start Page, click **New Project**. The New Project dialog box opens.

3. Click **Windows Forms Application**, and then click the **OK** button. The new project's Visual Studio Designer window opens. The Solution Explorer window tells you that, by default, this solution is named WindowsApplication1.

4. To give the solution a more meaningful name, click the name **WindowsApplication1** in the Solution Explorer window to select it, and then right-click the name. A pop-up menu opens.

5. On the pop-up menu, click **Rename**, type the new name Doubler, and then press the **Enter** key. In the Solution Explorer window, you can also see the form file named Form1.vb. We will not change this name.

Designing the Form for the Doubler Program

You must add three controls to the Doubler program's form: a textbox, a label, and a button, as shown in Figure 10-5. You have already seen a button, which is a control the user clicks to perform some action. You have also seen a label, which is a control that is used to display information. A **textbox** is a control that allows the user to enter input into a program. We use a textbox for user input (the number we want doubled) and a label to display information (the result of doubling the number).

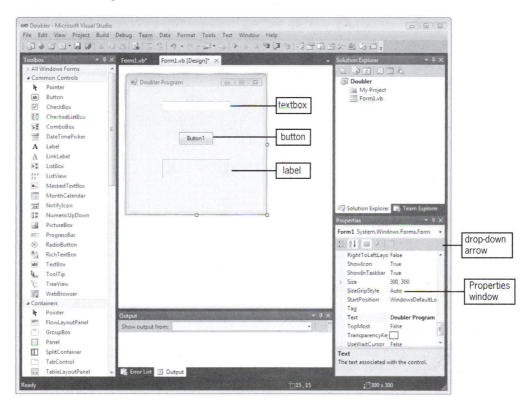

Figure 10-5 Doubler program form and controls

To add a textbox to the form:

1. Click **TextBox** in the Toolbox.

2. Move the mouse over the form to the position where you want to insert the textbox, using Figure 10-5 as a general guide.

3. Click and hold the left mouse button and then drag the pointer to draw a rectangle that roughly matches the size of the textbox in Figure 10-5.

 You may have to use the Toolbox scrollbar to scroll down to TextBox.

If you make a mistake, you can always select the textbox, delete it, and start over.

You may have to change one of the label properties to be able to size it as shown in Figure 10-5. This will be covered in the next section. For now, you can move on to the next step.

You learned about properties in Chapter 1 of this book.

The Name property represents the name of the control that you reference when you write Visual Basic code. The Text property represents the words that appear on the control. For example, the Text property of a form represents the words that appear on the title bar of the form.

4. Verify that the new textbox is located in the same position as the textbox in Figure 10-5. If necessary, move the mouse pointer over the middle of the textbox and drag the textbox to the desired location.

5. If the textbox does not match the size of the textbox in Figure 10-5, click the textbox (if necessary) to display the handles on its border, and drag one of the handles until the textbox is the desired size.

6. Use the **Label tool** in the Toolbox to add a label to the form. Follow the same basic steps that you used to add the textbox. When you're finished, your label should look like the one in Figure 10-5.

7. Use the **Button tool** in the Toolbox to add a button, using Figure 10-5 as a general guide. Move or resize the button, using the same procedure you used to adjust the textbox. When you're finished, your button should be the same shape and size as the button in Figure 10-5.

Now that you have placed the controls on the form, you can change some of their properties.

As shown in Figure 10-5, the Properties window is to the right of the Designer window. The **Properties window** provides access to a list of the properties and their values for all of the controls on the form, including the form itself. To alter properties, you must first select the appropriate control from the drop-down list at the top of the Properties window. A list of the current values for the properties for the selected control appears in the Properties window. Depending on what you clicked last when you were adding the controls to the form, it's possible that the form is currently selected. In the following steps, you start by selecting the form, just to make sure. Then you alter one of the form's properties.

1. Click the drop-down arrow at the top of the Properties window, and then click **Form1** in the drop-down list. The Properties window now displays the properties of the selected control (in this case, Form1).

2. Near the top of this Properties list, you see the Name property, which is currently set to Form1. In other words, the current value of the Name property is Form1. You will leave the Name property for Form1 unchanged, but you need to change the Text property to the text you want displayed in Form1's title bar.

3. Scroll to the Text property in the Properties window.

4. Click the **Text** property to select it, type Doubler Program and then press the **Enter** key. As shown in Figure 10-5, the words "Doubler Program" now appear on the title bar for Form1.

5. Take a moment to examine the Properties window, reviewing all the form's properties and their values.

Next, you change the name of the textbox from TextBox1 to the more meaningful name, txtInputNumber. Using descriptive names for the controls on a form makes it easier to keep track of the various controls in your code.

It is a Visual Basic convention to name controls using the first three characters of the name to identify the type of control, e.g., lbl for label controls, txt for textbox controls, and btn for button controls.

1. Select the textbox named **TextBox1** from the drop-down list.

2. In the Properties window, locate the Name property, click to select the Name property, type txtInputNumber, and then press the **Enter** key. You can leave the textbox's other properties unchanged.

Follow the same procedure to change properties of the button and the label as detailed in Table 10-1.

Control	Property	Value	Notes
Button1	Name	btnEnter	
	Text	Enter	
Label1	Name	lblAnswer	
	AutoSize	False	Click the down arrow and select **False** if it is not selected already. When the AutoSize property is set to True, the control is automatically sized to display its entire contents. When it is set to False, you can determine its size. You can now resize the lblAnswer label.
	BorderStyle	Fixed3D	Click the down arrow and select **Fixed3D** from the drop-down list.
	Text		Delete the word Label1 to clear the label of any text.

Table 10-1   Property values for button and label controls

When you are finished making the changes noted in Table 10-1, your form should look similar to the form shown in Figure 10-5 with one exception: the button should now display the text "Enter" rather than the text "Button1".

Writing the Code for the Doubler Program

When the Doubler program executes, it waits for the user to enter a number in `txtInputNumber` (the textbox) and then click on `btnEnter` (the button). When the user clicks on `btnEnter`, the program should double the number in `txtInputNumber` and display the result in `lblAnswer` (the label).

To write the code for this program, you must switch from the Designer window to the Code window. The quickest way to switch to the Code window is to double-click the control whose code you want to write. In this case, you want to write the code for the button control, so double-click the button `btnEnter` control now.

The Code window displays the following code:

```
Public Class Form1
    Private Sub btnEnter_Click( _
            ByVal sender As System.Object, _
            ByVal e As System.EventArgs) _
            Handles btnEnter.Click
    End Sub
End Class
```

The first line, `Public Class Form1`, and the last line, `End Class`, mark the beginning and end of a class that Visual Basic automatically creates for you. You learn more about classes in the next section of this chapter. For now, just keep in mind that this code is necessary and should not be changed. The second line of code is the header for a procedure named `btnEnter_Click`, and the `End Sub` in the second to last line is the procedure footer, which marks the end of the procedure. The header and footer for the `btnEnter_Click` procedure were automatically created by Visual Basic and should not be changed. Your job is to add code within the procedure. Notice that the procedure name consists of the control name (`btnEnter`) and the event name (`Click`) separated by an underscore (`_`). The code that you add to this procedure will execute when the user clicks the `btnEnter` control (also known as the "Enter" button).

An error occurs if you enter anything other than numeric values in the `txtInputNumber` textbox. You will learn how to handle this type of error as you learn more about Visual Basic.

You learned about the `Convert` methods in Chapter 2 of this book.

You want to retrieve the value the user entered by using the Text property of the textbox (`txtInputNumber`), multiplying it by 2, and then assigning it to the Text property of the label (`lblAnswer`). The following code shows you how to do this:

```
lblAnswer.Text = _

Convert.ToString(Convert.ToInt32(txtInputNumber.Text) * 2)
```

On the right side of the assignment statement, you retrieve the value of the Text property of the `txtInputNumber` textbox control, convert it to a numeric value using the `Convert.ToInt32()` method, and then multiply the converted numeric value by 2. The result is converted to a String and is then assigned to the Text property of the `lblAnswer` label control.

The Doubler program is now complete. Execute it a few times with different input values to test for correctness.

Exercise 10-1: Elements of a GUI in Microsoft Visual Studio

In this exercise, you use what you have learned about creating a GUI in Visual Studio to answer Questions 1–10.

1. Textboxes, buttons, and labels that are placed on a form are called _____.

2. A block of code that accomplishes a specific task is a(n) _____.

3. Write the Visual Basic statement that changes the color of the current form to green.

   _____

4. The mode of operation during which code can be executed is called _____.

5. The menu item to select to end run mode and return to design mode is _____.

6. What is a good name for a button with the word "Submit" on it? _____

7. In a GUI program, a(n) _____ causes a particular procedure to execute.

8. The window that lists all the controls, their properties, and their values is called the _____ window.

9. Controls are placed on a(n) _____.

10. The _____ displays the controls that you can add to your form.

LAB 10.1   Creating a Visual Basic GUI Program in Microsoft Visual Studio

In this lab, you create a Visual Basic GUI program in Microsoft Visual Studio. The program's form should include a textbox for user input and a button. When a user clicks the button, if a 1 is entered in the textbox, the background color of the form should change to red. If a 2 is entered, the background color of the form should change to yellow. If a 3 is entered, the background color of the form should change to green. If any value other than 1, 2, or 3 is entered, the background color of the form should be changed to white. Use the Gui Vote and the Doubler programs discussed in this chapter as guides. *Hint*: Use an `If Else If` statement in the click event procedure.

1. Open Microsoft Visual Studio, and create a new project named `Color Changer`.

2. Add the button and the textbox to the form in the Designer window, and change the properties of the form, the button, and the textbox as necessary.

3. Write the code for the button's click event.

4. Test the program.

5. Save the project as `Color Changer` in a directory of your choice.

A Programmer-Defined Class

Remember that attributes are called properties in Visual Basic.

You should do the exercises and labs in this section after you have finished Chapters 10 and 11 in *Programming Logic and Design, Sixth Edition*. You should also take a moment to review the object-oriented terminology (class, attribute, and method) presented in Chapter 1 of this book.

You have been using prewritten classes, objects, and methods throughout this book. For example, you have used the `System.Console.WriteLine()` method to display text. In this section, you learn how to create your own class that includes properties and methods of your choice. In programming terminology, a class created by the programmer is referred to as a **programmer-defined class**.

To review, procedural programming focuses on declaring data, defining procedures separate from the data, and then calling those procedures to operate on the data. This is the style of programming you have been using in Chapters 1 through 9 of this book. Object-oriented programming is different from procedural programming. Object-oriented programming focuses on an application's data and the methods you need to manipulate that data. The data and methods are **encapsulated**, or contained, within a class. Objects are created as an instance of a class. The program tells an object to perform tasks by passing messages to it. Such a message consists of an instruction to execute one of the class's methods. The class method then manipulates the data (which is part of the object itself).

Creating a Programmer-Defined Class

In Chapter 10 of *Programming Logic and Design, Sixth Edition*, you studied pseudocode for the Employee class. This pseudocode is shown in Figure 10-6. The Visual Basic code that implements the Employee class is shown in Figure 10-7.

```
 1 class Employee
 2     string lastName
 3     num hourlyWage
 4     num weeklyPay
 5
 6     void setLastName(string name)
 7         lastName = name
 8     return
 9
10     void setHourlyWage(num wage)
11         hourlyWage = wage
12         calculateWeeklyPay()
13     return
14
15     string getLastName()
16     return lastName
17
18     num getHourlyWage()
19     return hourlyWage
20
21     num getWeeklyPay()
22     return weeklyPay
23
24     void calculateWeeklyPay()
25         num WORK_WEEK_HOURS = 40
26         weeklyPay = hourlyWage * WORK_WEEK_HOURS
27     return
28 endClass
```

Figure 10-6 Pseudocode for Employee class

```
 1 Public Class Employee
 2
 3     Private Name As String
 4     Private Wage As Double
 5
 6
 7     Property LastName() As String
 8         Get
 9             Return Name
10         End Get
11         Set(ByVal Value As String)
12             Name = Value
13         End Set
14     End Property
15
16     Property HourlyWage() As Double
17         Get
18             Return Wage
19         End Get
20         Set(ByVal Value As Double)
21             Wage = Value
22         End Set
23     End Property
24
25     ReadOnly Property WeeklyPay() As Double
26         Get
27             Return Wage * 40
28         End Get
29     End Property
30 End Class
```

Figure 10-7 Employee class implemented in Visual Basic

To create the Employee class that will be used in a Visual Basic program named Employee Wages, first you build a form that looks like the one shown in Figure 10-8. Then, to create the Employee class:

1. Open the Add New Item dialog box by clicking **Project** and then clicking **Add Class**.

2. Click **Class**, then type Employee.vb in the Name textbox, and then click **Add**.

3. You will now see a new file appear in your project and a Code window within the Visual Studio IDE. In the Code window, there will be some code that looks like this:

```
Public Class Employee
End Class
```

All of the properties and methods that you create for this class must be entered between these lines of code.

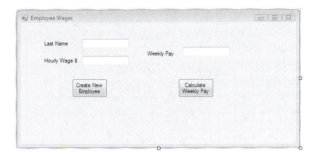

Figure 10-8   Form for the Employee Wages program

Looking at line 1 of the pseudocode in Figure 10-6, you see that you begin creating a class by specifying that it is a class. Looking at the Visual Basic code in Figure 10-7, you see that line 1 is the class declaration for the `Employee` class that begins with the keyword `Public`, which allows this class to be used in programs. The next word is the keyword `Class`, which specifies that what follows is a Visual Basic class. The `End Class` statement on line 30 marks the end of the class.

Adding Properties to a Class

The next step is to define the properties that are included in the `Employee` class. As shown on lines 2, 3, and 4 of the pseudocode in Figure 10-6, there are three attributes in this pseudocode class, `string lastName`, `num hourlyWage`, and `num weeklyPay`.

In Visual Basic, to create a property within a class, you can either create a `Public` field (variable) or you can create a private variable and expose the private variable using a `Property` statement. **Exposing** a variable means you make the variable available for use in a program. The following are advantages of exposing variables using a `Property statement`:

- You can create a read-only or write-only property, as opposed to a `Public` variable, which will always be read-write.

- You can expose calculated values as properties even if they are not stored as actual data within the class. An example of this is the `WeeklyPay` property. You probably don't want to store the weekly pay, as it could change.

Lines 3 and 4 in Figure 10-7 include two private variables, a `String` named `Name` and a `Double` named `Wage`. As explained in *Programming Logic and Design, Sixth Edition,* using the keyword `Private` means the data cannot be accessed by any method that is not part of the class. Programs that use the `Employee` class must use the methods that are part of the class to access private data.

Lines 7, 16, and 25 in Figure 10-7 include the `Property` statements in the Visual Basic version of the `Employee` class. These `Property` statements expose the private variables `Name` and `Wage` and also expose the calculated value `WeeklyPay`. Notice in the Visual Basic code that `HourlyWage()` and `WeeklyPay()` are defined using the `Double` data type, and `LastName()` is defined as a `String`. Also, notice that all three properties are written with parentheses following their names.

Adding Methods to a Class

The next step is to add methods to the `Employee` class. The pseudocode versions of these methods, shown on lines 6 through 27 in Figure 10-6, are nonstatic methods. As you learned in Chapter 10 of *Programming Logic and Design, Sixth Edition,* **nonstatic methods** are methods that are meant to be used with an object created from a class. In other words, to use these methods, we must create an object of the `Employee` class first and then use that object to invoke (or call) the method.

The code shown in Figure 10-7 shows how to include methods in the `Employee` class using Visual Basic. We will start the discussion with the set methods. You learned in *Programming Logic and Design, Sixth Edition,* that **set methods** are those whose purpose is to set the values of variables within the class. There are two private variables in the `Employee` class, `Name` and `Wage`, so we add two set methods, one for each of the two properties: `LastName` and `HourlyWage`.

The set method that begins on line 11 and ends on line 13 of Figure 10-7 executes when a value such as "Smith" is assigned to the `LastName` property of an `Employee` class object. You learn how to create an `Employee` class object and assign values to the object's properties later in this section. As you see on line 11, a single `String` argument, `Value`, is passed by value to this set method. On line 12, `Value` is assigned to the private variable named `Name`.

The set method that begins on line 20 and ends on line 22 executes when a value such as 25.00 is assigned to the `Wage` property of an `Employee` class object created in a Visual Basic program. As you see on line 20, a single `Double` argument, `Value`, is passed by value to the set method. On line 21, `Value` is assigned to the private variable named `Wage`. Remember that `WeeklyPay` is a calculated property and, therefore, does not require a variable to store its value and also does not require a set method.

The final step in creating the `Employee` class is adding the get methods. **Get methods** are methods that return a value to the program using the class. The pseudocode in Figure 10-6 includes three get methods: `getLastName()` on lines 15 and 16, `getHourlyWage()` on lines 18 and 19, and `getWeeklyPay()` on lines 21 and 22.

You can see the Visual Basic version of the three get methods in Figure 10-7. The get method that begins on line 8 and ends on line 10 executes when the value associated with the property LastName is retrieved. For example, a Visual Basic program may retrieve the value of the LastName property and then assign it to the Text property of a textbox. You will see a Visual Basic program that creates an Employee class object and then accesses the object's properties later in this section. As you see on line 8, there are no arguments passed to the get method, and on line 9, the value of the private variable Name is returned to the program.

The get method that begins on line 17 and ends on line 19 executes when the value associated with the property HourlyWage is retrieved. For example, a Visual Basic program may retrieve the value of the HourlyWage property and then assign it to the Text property of a textbox. As you see on line 17, there are no arguments passed to the get method, and on line 18, the value of the private variable Wage is returned to the program.

The get method that begins on line 26 and ends on line 28 executes when the value associated with the property WeeklyPay is retrieved. For example, a Visual Basic program may retrieve the value of the WeeklyPay property and then assign it to the Text property of a textbox. As you see on line 26, there are no arguments passed to the get method. On line 27, the value of the private variable Wage is multiplied by 40 to determine an employee's weekly pay, and then this calculated value is returned to the program. Notice this is a calculated property, which means there is no local variable that stores the value of an employee's weekly pay. Instead, the value is calculated by multiplying the employee's wage by 40 hours to determine the weekly pay.

The Employee class is now complete and may be used in a Visual Basic program.

As shown in Figure 10-8, there are three labels, three textboxes, and two buttons on the form. When a user clicks on the "Create New Employee" button, the Visual Basic program creates a new Employee object using the employee's last name and hourly wage entered in textboxes above the "Create New Employee" button. When a user clicks on the "Calculate Weekly Pay" button, the program calculates this Employee's weekly pay by multiplying the Employee's hourly wage by 40 hours and then displays the result in the textbox above the "Calculate Weekly Pay" button.

As shown in Figure 10-9, the Employee Wages program begins on line 1, with the creation of the class named Form1. On line 2, a reference to an `Employee` object is declared with the following statement:

```
Dim newEmp As Employee
```

```
 1 Public Class Form1
 2    Dim newEmp As Employee
 3    Private Sub btnNewEmployee_Click( _
 4            ByVal sender As System.Object, _
 5            ByVal e As System.EventArgs) _
 6            Handles btnNewEmployee.Click
 7
 8        newEmp = New Employee()
 9        newEmp.LastName = txtName.Text
10        newEmp.HourlyWage = Convert.ToDouble(txtHourly.Text)
11
12    End Sub
13
14    Private Sub btnWeekly_Click( _
15            ByVal sender As System.Object, _
16            ByVal e As System.EventArgs) _
17            Handles btnWeekly.Click
18        txtWeekly.Text = Format(newEmp.WeeklyPay, "Currency")
19    End Sub
20 End Class
```

Figure 10-9   Visual Basic code for the Employee Wages program

A **reference** is capable of storing the address in memory where an object is located. It is not the actual object.

On lines 3 through 12 of Figure 10-9, you see the `btnNewEmployee_Click()` event handler. On line 8, a new `Employee` class object (an instance of the `Employee` class) is created, and its address is assigned to `newEmp` using the following syntax:

```
newEmp = New Employee()
```

In Visual Basic, you create a new object by writing an assignment statement that consists of the object's name (`newEmp`) on the left side of the assignment operator and the `New` keyword followed by a constructor. In this example, the constructor is the class name (`Employee`) and a pair of empty parentheses. As you learned in *Programming Logic and Design,* a **constructor** is a method that creates an object. You also learned that you can use a prewritten **default constructor**, which is a constructor that expects no arguments and is created automatically by the compiler for every class you write. The `Employee()` constructor used in the Employee Wages program is an example of a prewritten default constructor.

Once the `newEmp` object is created, we can use `newEmp` to invoke the set methods to set the value of the `LastName` property to the value stored in the Text property of the textbox named `txtName` and the value of the `HourlyWage` property to the value stored in the Text property of the textbox named `txtHourly`. Notice the value stored in the Text property of the textbox named `txtHourly` is converted to a `Double` before it is assigned to the `HourlyWage` property. The correct syntax is shown in the following code sample:

```
newEmp.LastName = txtName.Text
newEmp.HourlyWage = Convert.ToDouble(txtHourly.Text)
```

Next, lines 14 through 19 implement the `btnWeekly_Click()` event handler. On line 18, `newEmp.WeeklyPay` is formatted as `Currency` using the `Format` function and then assigned to the Text property of the textbox named `txtWeekly`. Remember that accessing the `WeeklyPay` property invokes the get method for the `WeeklyPay` property.

You will find the completed program in a project named `EmployeeWages` included with the student files for this book.

Exercise 10-2: Creating a Class in Visual Basic

In this exercise, you use what you have learned about creating and using a programmer-defined class. Study the following code, and then answer Questions 1–4.

```
Public Class Circle

    Private rad As Double
    Const PI As Double = 3.14159

    Property Radius() As Double
        Get
            Return rad
        End Get
        Set(ByVal Value As Double)
            rad = Value
        End Set
    End Property

    ReadOnly Property Circumference() As Double
        Get
            Return 2 * PI * rad
        End Get
    End Property

    ReadOnly Property Area() As Double
        Get
            Return PI * rad * rad
        End Get
    End Property
End Class
```

In this exercise, assume that a `Circle` object named `myCircle` has been created in a program that uses the `Circle` class and that the radius of `myCircle` is 6.0.

1. What is the value stored in the textbox named `txtCircumference` when the following line of Visual Basic code executes?

    ```
    txtCircumference.Text = myCircle.Circumference
    ```

    _____

2. Assuming there is a textbox named `txtArea`, is the following a legal Visual Basic statement? Why or why not?

    ```
    txtArea.Text = Area()
    ```

    _____

3. Consider the following Visual Basic code. What is the value stored in the `myCircle` object's property named `Radius`?

    ```
    txtRadius.Text = 12.0
    myCircle.Radius = txtRadius.Text
    ```

    _____

4. Write the Visual Basic code that will assign the circumference of `myCircle` to a `Double` variable named `circumference1`.

    _____

LAB 10.2   Creating a Class in Visual Basic

In this lab, you create a programmer-defined class and then use it in a Visual Basic program. The program should create two `Rectangle` objects and find their area and perimeter. Use the `Circle` class that you worked with in Exercise 10-2 as a guide.

1. Create a project named `Rectangle` using Microsoft Visual Studio. (There is no student file for this Lab.)

2. Add a class named `Rectangle`, and in the `Rectangle` class, create two private variables named `len` and `wid`. Both `len` and `wid` should be data type `Double`.

3. Write the `Property` statements named `Length()` and `Width()` and the set methods to set the values for `len` and `wid`.

4. Write get methods to retrieve the values for `len` and `wid`.

5. Write an `Area()` `Property` statement and a `Perimeter()` `Property` statement to calculate and return the area of the rectangle and the perimeter of the rectangle.

6. Design a form that looks similar to the form shown in Figure 10-10.

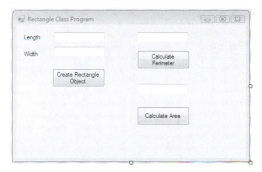

Figure 10-10   Rectangle program form

7. In the click event for the button labeled "Create Rectangle Object", create a `Rectangle` object named `newRect` and set the `Length` and `Width` properties of `newRect` to the width and the length entered in the textboxes associated with the length and the width of the rectangle.

8. In the click event for the button labeled "Calculate Perimeter", calculate `newRect`'s perimeter and assign it to the Text property of the textbox associated with the perimeter.

9. In the click event for the button labeled "Calculate Area", calculate `newRect`'s area and assign it to the Text property of the textbox associated with the area.

10. Save this project in a directory of your choice, and then make that directory your working directory.

11. Build the project named `Rectangle`.

12. Execute the program entering 4 for the length of the rectangle and 5 for the width of the rectangle. Calculate the perimeter and area of the rectangle.

13. Record the output displayed in the area and perimeter textboxes.

_____

_____

Index